Best Boss!

Best Boss!

The Impact of Extraordinary Leaders

Duncan Ferguson, Toni M. Pristo, and John Furcon

BEP

BUSINESS EXPERT PRESS

Leader in applied, concise business books

Best Boss!: The Impact of Extraordinary Leaders

First published in 2021 by
Business Expert Press, LLC
222 East 46th Street, New York, NY 10017
www.businessexpertpress.com

ISBN-13: 978-1-63742-322-6
ISBN-13: 978-1-63742-079-9 (e-book)

Business Expert Press Human Resource Management
and Organizational Behavior Collection

Collection ISSN: 1946-5637 (print)
Collection ISSN: 1946-5645 (electronic)

First edition: 2021

10 9 8 7 6 5 4 3 2 1

Description

This book pinpoints the one-on-one people leadership behaviors of extraordinary managers and provides strategies for developing the reader into a "Best Boss." Embedded in a model containing five dimensions, the Best Boss Approach presents a self-reinforcing and self-sustaining system of interaction, based on developing a foundation of trust and respect between manager and direct report that can last a lifetime. The book presents self-assessments and development tactics to facilitate growth in leadership insights and behavior. Moving beyond the individual leader, the authors examine factors within the organization that either promote or discourage "Best Boss" behaviors and suggest strategies for reducing barriers to successful leadership development. Finally, the book examines how the external market preoccupation and quest for shareholder value that is at odds with investments in leadership development and broader stakeholder value is now being reconsidered by economists and business leaders.

The book will be of singular assistance to anyone in a leadership role who manages people and aims to impact their motivation, engagement, performance, retention, and career development. It will also provide useful insights to leaders with responsibility for leadership development. Additionally, it provides significant value to two specific audiences: MBA students will find this book of particular value for shaping their leadership approach for enhancing business performance. CEOs and their advisors will find value in this book for gauging their organizations' current state of leadership development, readiness for improvement, and key areas of focus to achieve internal and external recognition as a "Best Boss" organization.

Keywords

leadership development; leadership; engagement; potential; trust; learning agility; organization improvement; values-based leadership; authenticity; individual performance

Contents

Testimonials

"'Best Boss! The Impact of Extraordinary Leaders' is focused on a topic that accounts for much of the variance in performance and satisfaction among people at work—in departments, teams, and organizations: what is the nature of boss-subordinate relations? When interactions are built on trust, as the authors explain, everyone wins. As an executive coach, I believe bosses can learn to build trust. For me, this book is valuable because it shows how."—**Harry Hutson, Executive Coach and Author of Navigating an Organizational Crisis: When Leadership Matters Most**

"When I look back upon the best bosses throughout my career, there were three recurring characteristics that inspired me to provide my best efforts: they were authentic in their approach, they cared for my well-being and they were generous in sharing their knowledge for my benefit. The best bosses generated more discretionary effort in my activities, I was grateful for their excellent care, and wanted to keep that partnership thriving. 'Best Boss! The Impact of Extraordinary Leaders' is a validation of my experience of great people leadership and what it can do for both employees and the organization."—**Bob Cancalosi, CEO and Owner of Four Loop Learning**

"'Best Boss! The Impact of Extraordinary Leaders' comes from a deep belief by the authors in the power of leadership and offers comprehensive research, assessments and self-reflection guides on effective behaviors. In addition, it encourages organizations to reflect on their mental models that underly and potentially interfere with leadership development. This book stirs your thinking and offers practical solutions."—**Malini Janakiraman , Malini Global Consulting**

"There are few things more important in our early growth and development than healthy attachments to our parents and caregivers. Similarly, there are few things as important in our work lives as who our supervisors are to us. What else has the degree of impact in terms of satisfaction and growth? Co-authors Duncan Ferguson, Toni Pristo and John Furcon have generated novel perspectives on best bosses which we know will be critically important. It will show how the workplace can be better for all of us. And for most of us work is where we will spend the better part of our lives."—**David Evan "Daven" Morrison, MD, Group for the Advancement of Psychiatry; Committee on Work and Psychiatry and author of Psychiatric Dysfunction in the Workplace (Oxford)**

"Having had the experience of working for a Best Boss, I know first-hand the immeasurable positive impact this type of leader can have on personal growth and professional progression. Working in the engagement space, I hear so many organizations and leaders wondering how managers and executives alike can drive engagement, innovation, and genuine connection — especially during this time where we are more remote than ever and increasingly burnt out. Ferguson, Pristo, and Furcon have harnessed the power of personal stories and consolidated them into universally relatable insights that inspire action. 'Best Boss! The Impact of Extraordinary Leaders' goes beyond description, helping readers reflect on their style through self-assessment exercises — allowing us all to realize our own personal brand of Best Bossing!"—**Carolyn Kalafut, MA, People Science Consultant at Glint, a part of LinkedIn**

"This isn't just a leadership book, it's a combination of powerful personal stories and insights that will stir emotion, inspire, and provide actionable strategies for becoming a Best Boss… a boss who brings out the best in others, activates potential, and makes the workplace experience (and the world) a truly better place. The Best Boss effect is hard to quantify… their impact can cascade through others in a way that multiplies their positive impact, creating more Best Bosses in the process. I've seen it firsthand in my work with organizations. Duncan, Toni, and John have poured their hearts and souls into the Best Boss research for years and this book brings their thought leadership to the world… grab a copy and get ready to be drawn right in…"—**Stefanie Mockler, Ph.D., Leadership Consultant, Coach and Founder of the Female Leader's Edge**

"You do not become a Best Boss overnight. This book will assist you in developing the skills and characteristics that make you an unforgettable leader … If you learn nothing else from reading this book, don't forget to reach out to your Best Boss and tell him or her how much of an impact they made in your work and personal life… and that you will continue this legacy."—**Paul Schneider, Partner, Keystone Partners**

Foreword

If you are looking for a quick read on how to become a "good enough" boss—one that doesn't inspire ridicule behind your back, well, you've come to the wrong place. Ferguson, Pristo, and Furcon set a much higher bar as they successfully distill the qualities and behaviors that distinguish extraordinary leaders from the rest of the pack. Their survey and related thinking focus on the women and men, from frontline supervisors to CEOs, who transcend their roles—shaping the very culture of the organizations they serve. Their positive influence on the individuals they manage is often surprisingly palpable and profoundly durable—they tend to leave an unforgettable mark. They are, by nature, talent magnets and talent actualizers, and it turns out there is a whole lot to learn from taking a closer look at how they succeed.

This work is clearly near and dear to the authors, which makes it all the more compelling. Each brings with them an entire career's worth of experience in studying, influencing, and indeed being led by the entire gamut of bosses, both strong and not-so-strong. Based on their survey results, which provide inspirational stories and powerful examples, they lay out a five-factor framework that is at once simple to grasp, yet profound in its impact. The pieces of the puzzle they identify are interdependent and complementary, transcending organizational settings, leadership levels and era. And, when they speak about "igniting the entire system," true magic emerges! Furthermore, they validate this model with related thinking from decades past. The good news is that reading "Best Boss! The Impact of Extraordinary Leaders" will most certainly inspire action. At the onset of the first page to the back cover, you'll be challenged constantly to engage in self-reflection and, more importantly, to do something different. The coaching they offer meets you where you are—early in your journey, or well down the path. All can benefit.

If you have managed to cross paths with a Best Boss, you have certainly been fortunate. You know firsthand how engaging and inspiring leaders like this can be. We need many more of them—now more than ever. Given the plethora of titles out there in the "make-a-better-leader" industry that don't exactly live up to their promise, it's about time one shoots for the stars and actually hits the mark.

Carl Robinson, PhD
Founding Partner, Vantage Leadership Consulting
Chicago, Illinois

Preface

Reflecting on our careers, we are very much aware of the fact that a small handful of people have had a disproportionate impact on our success. Some have been colleagues or peers; some have been teachers, coaches, or even clients. And then there are those cases in which our own manager greatly affected the trajectory of our lives. A few years back, we discussed the idea of taking a more substantive look at the method and impact of these inspiring individuals by learning how others would respond to two straightforward yet provocative queries:

- Who was your "Best Boss?"
- Why do you think so?

The study that followed these two questions yielded profound insights in terms of who a Best Boss is, what he or she does, and the subsequent impact of such leadership.

The reader might wonder why our efforts were directed at understanding a "boss" rather than a manager, supervisor, or even leader. If so, you are not alone—for at least one of our book reviewers, Harry Hutson, did the same:

> In today's world, hierarchy is blurred, except in repetitive work-flows. Knowledge and service workers work independently or in teams where their colleagues, peers, outside experts, and even clients are more important than their direct supervisors. Does the boss concept even fit?

In fact, as we set up the study, it was not a consideration we took lightly. We tested the use of the term "boss" in advance and found that it resonated clearly with all ages and generations. The common interpretation is that a boss is someone who has a big impact on one's life at work, both in reference to the conduct of the work itself, and with reference to the leadership style an individual enjoyed (or endured). It wasn't just about managing, supervising, or leading—it was about all of these things. "Boss" fit the bill.

Much of what we have learned has been deciphered from the stories that came as a result of our research methodology. These stories conveyed not only the behaviors and traits of respondents' Best Bosses, but also the emotion elicited in working with him or her. For some, the recollections were, at times, overwhelming, even in instances where decades had passed.

In reality, very few of the Best Bosses we studied seemed to come close to being perfect. However, what stood out as common denominators among a highly diverse set of individuals deemed a Best Boss, was each one's unique way of:

- Establishing a positive connection and authentic relationship with the individual; and
- Creating an environment in which a person was encouraged to reach his or her potential, that, in turn, benefitted the organization.

As authors, we anticipated the positive impact of a Best Boss, but upon reflection, we found the topic even more compelling in the context of the world in which we live today. Writing this book during the summer of 2020, a sense of urgency developed around our mutual mission to complete it, as global events unfolded around us with dramatic ramifications for life as we know, or knew it:

- The COVID-19 virus is changing both how we work and how we collaborate.
- The Black Lives Matter movement has resulted in organizations re-examining how we relate to, work with, and lead others equitably.
- Political developments brought the question of leadership to the forefront on a daily basis.
- The Me-Too movement demanded the eradication of all sexual harassment and abuse in the workplace and in life.

- Leading up to 2020, newer generations of workers, led by Millennials, had already begun to demand that organizations evolve in how they both operate and integrate into our work and lives.
- The evolution of social media and its impact on our work life and everyday life is an experiment in progress.

So, what is the impact of a Best Boss and why is this way of leading so urgently needed at this turbulent time in modern history? Through our efforts and reflections, we learned that a Best Boss elicited a level of commitment and conviction within a person that ensured he or she would consistently go beyond ordinary performance at work. And more, the effect of a Best Boss was often to create "leadership legacies"— generating a multiplier effect in the sense that, great bosses beget great bosses.

Beyond that, we believe the most important effect of the Best Boss way of leading is the impact it can have on the human condition—by reducing the stress and demoralization of disengagement, by always encouraging respect and integrity, and by showing us through their interactions that each and every one of us matters, at work and in life. This bold statement will reveal its own explanation in the stories that lie ahead. Consider this book a different kind of leadership exploration, as it addresses the human experience between two people, not just the work experience.

Best Boss! The Impact of Extraordinary Leaders is offered for those who are looking for a way to make a meaningful difference through the way they lead others in this challenging and chaotic world. Such individuals likely understand the value of great people leadership, but may not be so clear as to how to bring it about, whether that be in the employees they currently lead or in anticipation of future leadership roles to which they aspire. We believe our characterization and approach to leading as a Best Boss are timeless, no matter the era and are blind to race, culture, or differences in sexual orientation. This is because, amid the chaos that always accompanies large-scale change, transition and the human condition, people yearn for compassion, support, and authenticity in their work and their lives.

In *Best Boss! The Impact of Extraordinary Leaders*, we will share a systemic approach to the Best Boss way of leading, some of which might already be incorporated into your current leadership style. We will describe specific traits, behaviors, and tools, as well, for both your reflection and use in unleashing your own unique capabilities. In doing so, we invite you to join us on this journey of discovery and discernment to embolden your leadership and be ready to take on the possibilities of tomorrow.

> *If your actions inspire others to dream more, learn more, do more and become more, you are a leader.*
> —Quote attributed to John Quincy Adams, the sixth president
> of the United States

Acknowledgments

Duncan Ferguson

So many people, once they learned about our Best Boss study and associated insights, have asked me, "So, when are you writing a book?" However, writing a book is much harder than it looks. It took incredible support and assistance from so many special people that I would be remiss for not acknowledging their participation in this achievement.

First, and most importantly, I am forever grateful to my wife, Linda, who told me from the beginning to stop thinking about writing and *just write*! Many in my family were also so interested in the Best Boss effort, from my sons, Ryan and Brendan to my Canadian family, Karen, John, Ken, Lauren, William, Beth Anne, Janet, and Paul.

None of this, from the Best Boss study and analysis, could have happened without the friendship, thought leadership and avid interest from all of the folks at Vantage Leadership Consulting. Cat Savage was there from the beginning, playing a pivotal role in our data gathering and analysis. Lees Parkin provided her story, literary elegance, and continual enthusiasm. Stephanie Mockler, Eileen Linnabery, Kelly Levin, and Kathy Kurnyta took the lead in developing our Best Boss workshops. Last, and not least, are the partners at Vantage—Carl Robinson, Keith Goudy, Mike Tobin, Jackie Ackerman, and Dave Sowinski, who were encouraging, supporting, curious, and nurturing throughout.

Special thanks to Rich McGourty for his keen insights, artful criticism, and ever-present optimism.

A big shout out to our extended team member and editor, Lizzie Riggan, who did a spectacular job polishing our thoughts and making us look like actual writers.

Thanks to the provocateurs, Phil Gardner, Paul Schneider, and Phil Kosanovich, who continually queried, "when is that book going to be done?"

To all of my corporate Best Bosses (yes, I was lucky to have many) who made my work strong and my whole life brighter through their coaching, "potential activation," and friendship. Thanks to Melanie Brennan, Wendell Johnson, Joe Ryan, Ed Van Steddam, Jack Graham, Bill Slight, Henry Davis, Kent Carson, Doug Ford, Dave Lemmon, Carol Bullock, John Campbell, Wayne Anderson, and Tobi D'Andrea.

To all of our survey respondents, too numerous to name, but who took the time to provide such thoughtful, robust, and inspirational stories about their own Best Bosses. Their quotes provided the heart and soul to our book.

Finally, to my two coauthors, a deep and heartfelt thank you to Toni and John, who have been on this journey with me from the beginning. Without their friendship, expertise, passion, and resilience, none of this would have happened.

Toni Pristo

I would like to acknowledge coauthors Duncan and John for our collaboration on the topic of Best Boss. Between a recession and a pandemic, we conducted the Best Boss study and eventually wrote a book, thus creating opportunities to do meaningful work during particularly difficult times. Plus, we had fun. In addition to comments already made about Vantage, I also wanted to call out Cat Savage for her impeccable work on developing and maintaining the study database. What a difference it has made for us! When it comes to book content, I have to thank my original Best Bosses—Tony and Margie Pristo. Their parenting method was analogous to and inspirational for understanding a Best Boss. Heartfelt thanks to BEP's Scott Isenberg, Mike Provitera and Charlene Kronstedt who lifted us through the publishing process with such validation, not to mention alacrity. Finally, I must thank Best Boss Warren Wilhelm who routinely "activates employee potential." For me, he suggested I start my own consulting business—something I never would have imagined. As of this publication, it is in its 25th year. More importantly, having my own business enabled the life I so desired with my family for whom I am the most grateful—Dan, Michael and Gina Conti.

John Furcon

First and foremost, especial thanks to my coauthors, Toni and Duncan, who demonstrated remarkable insight, diligence, eloquence, and working from "higher purpose" throughout our journey from research to publication. In addition to the preceding affirmations of Vantage staff and other colleagues who supported our work, three other individuals stand out for me: Alan Tecktiel (HR executive) who supported our initial foray into implementation of a Best Boss workshop and diagnostic 360-degree feedback process, which provided the unvarnished reactions of potential users to our ideas; Kathleen Quinn (film producer), who directed our quest into capturing CEO video reminiscences of Best Boss experiences; and Harry Hutson (executive coach), who reviewed our draft manuscript and conveyed many substantive observations which challenged our thinking and honed our insights and writing.

I've been fortunate to have a number of great bosses. Four individuals, however, were singular in this regard at different stages of my career: Wally (Wallace) Lonergan at the Human Resources Center, The University of Chicago; Bea Young at Harbridge House, and Bud Block and Iris Goldfein at PriceWaterhouseCoopers. They personified quite memorable facets of Best Boss behavior in their leadership and in our work relationships.

I realize that learning from the work experiences of family members has had a decided impact on my views of and insights concerning the boss-employee relationship. Being blessed with five daughters and five sons-in-law (Juliana and Pete, Annalisa and Phil, Diana and Gary, Sarah and Adam, Beth and Chris) who have freely shared ideas and experiences from their career journeys, I feel that a multigenerational perspective has been "baked in" along the way. Additional learning, courtesy of our eight grandchildren, is underway.

Finally, my heartfelt thanks to my wife, Denise Bettenhausen, whose encouragement and support was incredibly important to me throughout the authorship process. In addition, her career as an educational administrator and consultant has provided many relevant experiences and insights that she has generously shared. In truth, I suspect that many of her colleagues and workmates would describe her as a Best Boss! And her comments on the final draft were most helpful in bringing the book to completion.

Introduction

We did not discover the topic of Best Bosses as an outgrowth of a pre-determined academic pursuit to uncover the secrets of great leadership. It germinated rather from a simple comment to Duncan, made by an individual named Joel as he was describing why he loved his current job:

> It's because of my boss. He is absolutely the best boss I have ever had in my life. I am given autonomy and freedom to run my business unit. He gives me constructive feedback when necessary and recognition when warranted. He has my back in all situations. And he really cares about me as a person. I don't think I will ever be able to work for anyone else again because this experience has been so great.

While Joel's description of his boss was intriguing, it was his last sentence that catches one's attention. Joel assumed it was unlikely he would find another great boss during his career. In other words, having a great boss was the *exception*, not the rule, in employees' working lives.

Duncan Ferguson

As a human resources leader and then organizational consultant, Duncan has been fascinated with understanding the secrets of great leadership throughout his entire career. But the conversation with Joel was a catalyzing event. Shortly thereafter, Duncan began to casually incorporate the question, "Who was your Best Boss?" into interactions with friends, business colleagues, and clients. The responses were universally positive, emotional, and energizing. He also created a leadership blog in hopes of collecting more evidence for the importance of this topic. One comment from a reader stands out:

The greatest boss EVER … he cared about everyone in his department. He had extreme competence and was trusted by most important people above him. But really it all came down to giving you a clear direction and, within that, complete autonomy. He didn't allow "run-arounds" by his direct reports, stuck up for you with your peers and other departments, and if he didn't agree with you, he dealt with you in private and let you sort things out. He had an open door and always made you feel welcome when you came in to talk with him.

Invigorated by these interactions, Duncan connected with Toni and John, as he was aware of their shared passion for the topic.

Toni Pristo

As an organizational psychologist, Toni's interest and work in the area of leadership behavior and effectiveness at multiple organizational levels has spanned a long career. In a variety of internal and external roles she has played as an organization and leadership development consultant, the topic of boss–employee relationships has been a strong focus. Equally important, she also has abundant experiences—and memories—of her own bosses who, from her perspective, ran the gamut from not-so-good to out of this world. Trying to understand this great divide, the inconsistency of great boss leadership in organizations, and the role of the "other" in the boss employee relationship hold unending interest.

For years, Toni worked with first-time "people leaders" to develop emotional competence as a way to optimize boss–employee relationships. In a specially designed exercise, workshop participants would begin to understand the difference between "good" and "bad" bosses by collectively recalling their own past experiences. After dividing the class into two groups—one that experienced a great boss and one that experienced an undesirable boss—the two subgroups collected the following data:

- What did the boss say or do?
- How did it make you feel?
- What was the impact on performance—yours, your team, your organization?

Inevitably, the two groups learned rather quickly the correlation between boss behaviors, employee feelings, and impact on performance. For example, a boss who shouted at a direct report intimidated the employee, and performance diminished out of fear of making mistakes. On the other hand, a boss who openly recognized a deserving employee made the individual feel confident, which in turn, translated into enhanced future performance due to growing confidence and developing trust with the boss.

Certainly, emotional intelligence and competence were central to the Best Boss–employee relationship. But what else? A chance reunion with two colleagues from the very beginning and middle of her career would provide an interesting opportunity to find out.

John Furcon

John, also an organizational and leadership consultant, has demonstrated a career-long interest in great leadership. It began with developing and validating psychological tests and assessment centers for manager selection, and continued with design and implementation of 360-degree feedback, management development, and succession planning programs. However, he recognized that great leadership involved more than just the sum of strong competencies. This seemed to be the case at all levels in organizations, from first-line supervisors up to and including C-Suite officers and CEOs. Other, more intangible processes seemed to be in play.

John's attraction to the topic of Best Bosses was also more organic and even personal. Early in his career, he recognized the importance of having a great boss from whom he could learn; one who would trust and respect him. As he moved through his career, he was fortunate to have several great bosses who met these standards, supporting him to perform effectively in making a positive impact on organizations and people. One story in particular is emblematic of the impact a Best Boss can have:

> It was my first interview with my prospective boss when I was making the career transition from academia to consulting. I arrived with a briefcase filled with papers, publications, and reports, which at one point, I began to spread out on the desk for her review. I remember clearly the moment she interrupted me and made a statement to the effect of "There's no need to look at any of that; we look forward to learning from you and providing the opportunity for you to put these approaches to use in the organizations we assist."

It is hard to imagine a more positive start to a new career direction.

Our Journey of Discovery Begins

Ultimately, the three of us gathered at a suburban Chicago coffee shop where we discussed our mutual interest in discovering the exceptional aspects of a Best Boss. We also discussed, based on our collective 100+

years of human resources and consulting experience, a shared viewpoint on the general state of leadership across all types of public and private organizations. At best, we felt the current state of leadership was uninspired. At worst, we thought it was horrible. And, we believed that most of us were feeling the fallout.

The numbers support this anecdotal point of view on leadership. Consider these data points from Gallup (State of the American Workforce Report 2020):

- Only 33 percent of employees are engaged in their work and workplace.
- Just 20 percent of employees say their performance is managed in a way that motivates them to do outstanding work.
- Fifty-six percent of nonengaged and 73 percent of actively disengaged employees are looking for jobs or watching for opportunities.
- Three in 10 of U.S. employees say they have received praise or recognition for good work in the past seven days.
- Three in 10 of U.S. employees say there is someone at work who encourages their development.
- Four in 10 of U.S. employees say that their supervisor or someone at work cares about them as a person.

If these data aren't depressing enough, there is ample evidence—to be shared later in the book—that your boss also has an immediate impact on your personal health and well-being.

Our own intrigue with the topic, coupled with years of discouraging data on the state of work, motivated us to better understand what differentiates a Best Boss from all others. But before we dive into what this book is, we feel it important to tell you what it isn't.

It would have made sense if Joel's story led us to take a closer look at bad bosses. After all, bad bosses are, in their own right, alluring. Who among us hasn't heard or shared a funny (or painful) story about a toxic boss? We decided, however, to go in a more positive direction and set out to study Best Bosses, like the one Joel was fortunate enough to have, rather than the terrible bosses that many of us have had to endure from time to time throughout our careers. This is not unlike the notion that in order to understand why some marriages are great, it makes more sense to study successful marriages, rather than those that end in divorce. While certain topics are of critical import for further research and discussion at this particular time in modern history, the following considerations are not directly addressed in this book: the employee–boss relationship with respect to gender, race, and sexual orientation. We strongly support the exploration of such topics. At the same time, we entertain the possibility that so many issues in the workplace might disappear on their own if we lived in a world in which Best Boss leadership was the rule, and not the exception. In this regard, all employees, regardless of race, gender, or orientation might feel the psychological space at work to be, and continue becoming, the best version of themselves. We understand this vision is an extremely tall order and do. not discount for a moment the unacceptable situations endured by far too many for far too long: biases in leadership based on such factors cannot be tolerated in organizations. Period.

Overview of the Book

Now, on to what this book is and what we hope it will provide for our reader. The book begins with a story, based on a late entry to our study, that sets the stage for what it means and feels like to have a Best Boss. This first story is about Courtney, a Gen-Xer. Two more stories—not from our study, but from our direct experience in working with others—are told in the middle and end of the book. They are based on the experiences of a Baby Boomer (Jeff) and a Millennial (Lees). This is one way in which we attempt to demonstrate that this type of leadership has universal impact, regardless of age.

Chapter 2 ("A Simple Study") provides a detailed look at our Best Boss study design and methodology as well as an initial look at some findings such as study demographics, traits, and overall themes describing the purview of Best Boss leadership. In Chapter 3, the reader is presented with a model of how the employee–Best Boss interaction seems to operate, and the impact it has for each individual and the organization as a whole. Chapters 4 through 8 cover an in-depth look at Best Boss behaviors. They include an abundance of quotes gathered from the research we conducted that led us to develop the models and tools offered in this book. In addition, these chapters include references to other important research where similar findings have been identified. Finally, these chapters also provide the reader with an opportunity to begin a self-reflection journey in regards to how well he or she currently behaves in the fashion of a Best Boss. In Chapter 9, the reader will discover methods for assessing current leadership capabilities, and it also provides suggestions for what he or she can do to address needed improvements.

Throughout earlier chapters, there are many references to the importance of Best Boss leadership. Chapter 11, Why Best Bosses Matter, takes a deeper dive into the "why" and will reference compelling evidence for the pursuit of great leadership that goes well beyond what we have identified. Chapter 12 presents considerations as to why Best Bosses are few and far between and concludes the discussion with hopeful developments to address these issues, as well as how our audience might intervene within their own organization, if leadership deficits exist. We sincerely hope that our readers will find inspiration for championing and becoming a Best Boss in reading this book.

.

CHAPTER 1

Courtney's Story: Perspective of a GenXer

Courtney was 21, recently out of college, and ready to get her career and life started. Following graduation from Vanderbilt, she landed a position in Chicago as a research analyst at a professional services firm. Courtney was filled with a host of emotions as she entered the workforce—excitement, anticipation, anxiety, hope. While she believed in herself and knew she was capable, she was also confronted with the typical self-doubt and uncertainty that accompanies any big transition. And she was experiencing plenty of firsts in her life—new job, new city, new expectations. Perhaps the most intimidating "first" for Courtney was working for a real boss. It's not that Courtney had never been supervised before, but only on summer or part time jobs. This, however, was a real job with a real boss, someone who would set her objectives, judge her performance, and permeate a significant portion of her life. The prospect distressed her.

With these anxieties firmly in tow, Courtney began working for Bob, a senior project manager at her firm. Almost immediately, Courtney realized her concerns were unfounded. Bob disarmed her by being genuinely interested in her as an individual. He appreciated how difficult it can be to start a new job—especially early in one's career—and he made it his mission to help her be successful at the firm.

Bob brought many great human qualities to their working relationship. He was a coach, mentor, confidant, and ultimately, a friend. From the very beginning of their time working together, Bob made it clear that he fully trusted Courtney and truly valued her judgement. Even though Courtney was young and unproven, he immediately sought to collaborate with her and encouraged her to share her opinions.

Whether introducing her to new experiences, providing access to strategic conversations with clients, or creating developmental opportunities,

Bob quickly became Courtney's strongest advocate. Occasionally, he would "push" Courtney outside of her comfort zone, which could be uncomfortable for her. One memorable experience occurred when Bob and his team were preparing for a global conference to be attended by 100 of the firm's top senior consultants. Since she was still relatively new in her role, Courtney assumed she would simply provide background support for the conference. She was wrong.

While discussing the agenda during a preplanning meeting, Bob mentioned that he was going to give Courtney the opportunity to lead an important topic discussion. Her heart rushed to her throat. Did she hear him right? What was he thinking, placing a young, inexperienced person in front of such a high-powered group? She never would have sought out such an assignment on her own. But Bob, well aware of her anxiety, immediately helped assure her by saying, "you are going to get up there, own this time, and do a great job." Courtney was not so sure, but Bob's encouragement bolstered her. As the conference date approached, Courtney was scared, to be sure, but she was also gaining confidence. After all, if Bob believed in her, maybe she should as well! When the big day finally arrived, Courtney was nervous as her time on the agenda approached. There was no saving her now, but as she got to the front of the room, she looked out into the audience to see Bob smiling, giving her give her a thumbs up salute. The presentation went flawlessly, and as Courtney recounts,

> When you know someone believes in you, provides a safety net, encourages you to do your best and reminds you it's okay to not be perfect, your fear melts away and you can do just about anything.

There were occasions, however, when Courtney would put Bob's faith in her to the test. One such instance, from early on in her time working for Bob, still stands out in her memory. During her first few weeks on the job, Courtney was given an assignment to oversee a marketing project to create and then mail an important communication to a list of critical customers and potential future clients. Before the communication was released, Bob reviewed it with the CEO, who quickly pointed out that the first client name on the communication was completely misspelled.

Thousands of copies of the communication had already been printed and were scheduled for mailing later that day. After finding out what happened, Courtney was mortified. She walked, well... actually it was more like a hurried trot... to Bob's office with the intention of offering a heartfelt apology. She fully expected a good "chewing out" or worse. Either way, it felt like the end of the world. Or at least it did, until she arrived at Bob's door where he reassured her that, "These things happen, and this is not the worst thing that is going to happen in your life. Everything is going to be okay." Years later, Courtney still thinks back to this particular incident. It's funny how early career mistakes never totally leave your consciousness. But more importantly, what also stuck with Courtney was how Bob defused the situation with kindness and reassurance. It was a moment she will always remember.

Courtney recognized the impact Bob had on both her performance and her career as a whole. She excelled, both personally and professionally, during her time with him. This was driven, in part, by his support, but there were other parts of his leadership style that brought out the best in her, too. He consistently empowered Courtney to be innovative, to try new things, and to take risks. He regularly adjusted her role to keep it both interesting and developmental.

Perhaps the biggest influence Bob had on Courtney was via the values-based behaviors he displayed at work. Bob was resolute in his commitment to both the customer and the people who worked under his supervision. He was also committed to doing quality work. Bob was always true to his word by being reliable, trustworthy, transparent, and honest. These were natural traits for Bob, and it was impossible for Courtney not to be impacted by such integrity. As Courtney reflects on her relationship with Bob, she can easily see the direct line between Bob and her own values and leadership behaviors. Commitment, quality, trust, and integrity have become themes for her, both in work and in life in general.

Bob and Courtney's lives eventually diverged. He continued with the company, advancing to more senior level roles during his tenure. Courtney's life expanded. She moved on to different jobs and ultimately different companies, earned her master's degree, got married, and became a mother. They eventually lost touch with each other, until the day a friend reached out to her and asked her for favor. He wondered if Courtney had ever been lucky enough to have a Best Boss, and, if so, would she take a moment to complete a survey on her experience? Intrigued, she kept the e-mail, fully intending to follow through on the request when she had a moment to reflect. But life intervened and she forgot about the request until she stumbled upon it in her inbox a few weeks later. When she opened the survey, memories of Bob came rushing back. Each question joyfully made her remember a wonderful man who she was lucky enough to have as her first boss. Here is how she completed the survey:

Why do you consider this person your favorite boss?
"He is the whole package! An inspirational leader, a mentor, a friend and one of my greatest advocates and supporters. He is very dear to me…like a second father."

What kinds of things would he/she say or do?
"As Practice Leader and Consultant, he was a strong, decisive, strategic leader who took care of the people who worked for him, while still enabling them to be independent and grow. He highly valued my thinking, judgment and input and solicited it often in making decisions. This was empowering. He believed in my potential and opened doors for me into new experiences, roles, and opportunities. He always had my best interests in mind, and his actions spoke as loudly as his words."

How did this person make you feel?
"Empowered, smart, capable, supported, and safe."

What were the impacts on your career to this point?
"Bob has played a tremendous role in instilling many of the values I bring to my work each day. A strong client focus, a commitment to quality, and following through on my commitments to myself, my colleagues, and my clients."

Please provide at least one story or specific experience that stands out in your memory as an example of why this person is your favorite boss. Please indicate what the person said or did. Also describe how it made you feel.

"Early in my career, I was working on a marketing piece 'announce-ment card' that was sent to all of the firm's clients, which included many C-Level executives from companies across the Fortune 1000. After thousands of copies had been printed and were at the mail house about to be distributed, the Chairman of our firm pointed out to Bob that the name of one of our key clients was prominently misspelled on the very front page. Somehow, I had missed it! I felt absolutely terrible, was sick to my stomach, and told Bob to take the cost of the printing out of my bonus. I thought he would be angry, but much to my surprise, he was understanding and forgiving. It's a small story and gesture, but I will never forget the level of compassion and support he showed me. It made me realize that it was safe to make mistakes working for him, and that he would always have my back. He knew I was doing the best I could, that I was fully committed to my role and to delivering a quality product, and also that I was human…and he supported me, despite my mistake."

What would you tell that person today if you had the chance to see him/her in person?
"Thank you!!!! Words cannot express what your support, mentor-ship, guidance, and friendship have meant to me all of these years. I would not be the professional or person I am today without you and all you have given me. I am incredibly grateful, appreciative and privileged to have known and worked with you. I will take everything you have taught me into all of my future roles in work and life as a colleague, friend, wife, and mother."

The last question lingered with Courtney as she wistfully recalled a special person who had made a such an imprint on her life. Had she ever told him? She did not think so. Yet, even if she had, the time had come to give proper thanks. So, Courtney set off to reconnect with Bob. Through her network, she discovered Bob had retired and was still living in the same house he called home during their days working together. She also learned the unimaginable—that Bob had a terminal illness and did not have long to live. Wasting no time, Courtney printed a copy of her sur-vey responses and headed to the hospital to tell Bob, in person, what he meant to her. Upon arrival, she was told that Bob was too sick to receive visitors. Distraught, but undaunted, she gave the document to Bob's wife with the attached note:

I was recently asked to be interviewed regarding my favorite boss, who is resoundingly YOU. I felt like my responses truly captured all that you mean to me and the multitude of ways you have touched and enriched my life over the years, so I've enclosed the transcript for you to see. It could never do justice to expressing the role you've played in my life and the special place you hold in my heart, but it's a start. I hope you find comfort and peace knowing how many people love you and the level of positive impact you've had on everyone you've touched in this world.

Love always,
Courtney

A short time later, Bob died. But before he did, his wife had the opportunity to share Courtney's words of admiration and love with him. Bob's family was so moved by Courtney's testimonial that excerpts were shared at his funeral, and there wasn't a dry eye in the gathering as her words were read.

CHAPTER 2

A Simple Study

Introduction

Much of the impetus for our interest in this topic is rooted in personal experiences with our own supervisors and managers, as well as our education and professional experiences. We wondered if we could identify traits, commonalities, or patterns of behavior that were consistently linked to the Best Boss experiences of a variety of people. We hoped that our work would identify teachable skills that would assist people in becoming better leaders. To formalize our shared commitment, we even established a new organization to serve as the repository of our research data, findings and conclusions. We call it Lead Well, LLC.

Data Collection

Our first step was to design a data collection process. Rather than attempt some sort of numerical rating of preconceived behaviors or experiences, we developed a set of open-ended survey questions that would allow respondents to provide descriptions and examples of their boss' behaviors and the impact of their Best Boss experience on their own performance and career (see Figure 2.1). In addition, we included a few demographic questions to help us characterize our respondent population by gender, business function, experience, and career stage.

Assisted by Vantage Leadership Consulting, LLC, we established a website to host our questionnaire and then proceeded to advise colleagues by e-mail of the research project and the opportunity to participate. We also encouraged them to invite other interested parties to participate. Over a period of several months, we gathered at total of fifty-five complete and usable online replies—a sufficient database for an exploratory study of this nature.

)PINIONS FROM THE EMPLOYEE PERSPECTIVE: Answe.
ach question by typing your response in the space provided.

o you have a favorite boss? If so, please take a minute, review the following question:
nd share your thoughts about this very important person.

1. Why do you consider this person your favorite boss?
2. What kinds of things woulds he/she say or do?
3. How did this person make you feel?
4. What were the impacts on
   a. Your performance at the time?
   b. Your career to this point?
5. Please provide at least one story or specific experience that stands out in your memory as an example of why this person is your favorite boss. Please indicate what the person said or did. Also describe how it made you feel.
6. What would you tell that person today if you had the chance to see him/her in person?
7. Would you be interested in being interviewed in person about these experience to contribute to a video archive of "favorite boss" leadership practices?

Figure 2.1 Best boss online questionnaire content

Analysis of Respondent Demographics

Sixty-three percent of respondents were male and 34 percent were female.

Figure 2.2 presents the career tenure breakdown of respondents. The majority (60 percent) had been working for at least twenty years, providing ample time for both exposure to different supervisors, as well as opportunity to develop perspective on the role and leadership practices of a boss.

Figure 2.3 presents the career stage of respondents. Roughly one-third (35 percent) described themselves as being early in their career, 40 percent as mid-career, and the balance (23 percent) as late career. Thus, the complete range of career lifecycle experience is represented in our data.

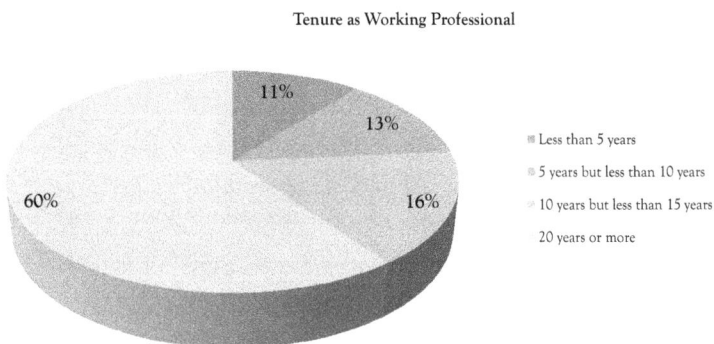

Tenure as Working Professional

11%

13%

60%   16%

▩ Less than 5 years

◉ 5 years but less than 10 years

◌ 10 years but less than 15 years

20 years or more

Figure 2.2 Career tenure breakdown of respondents

Career Stage

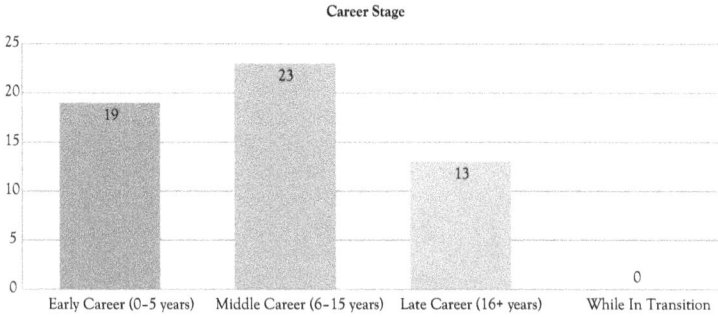

Figure 2.3 Career stage breakdown of respondents

Note: Numbers embedded in bar charts indicate the number of study participants.

With respect to leadership level (Figure 2.4), the majority (42 percent) were individual contributors, 35 percent were managers of individual contributors, and the balance (23 percent) were managers of multiple levels and/or functions, providing a reasonable sample of perspectives across levels of managerial responsibility.

As shown in Figure 2.5, the majority (49 percent) identified human resources as their primary functional area of responsibility, with the balance spread over at least eight other areas of business function. All in all, the sample represents considerable breadth and depth of an organizational experience, and aside from an overrepresentation of the HR function, a wide range of business function backgrounds.

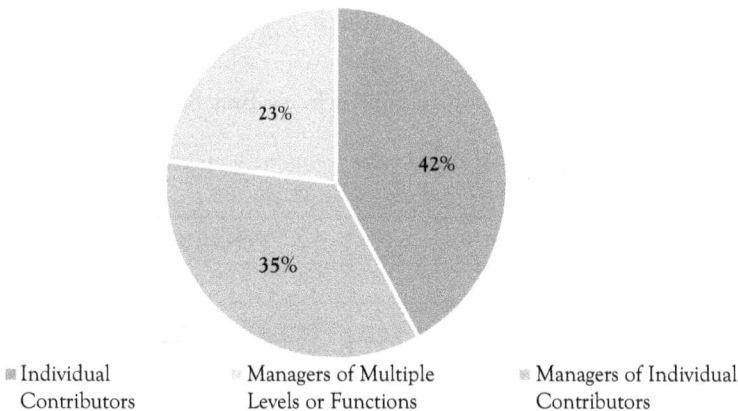

Figure 2.4 Leadership level breakdown of respondents

Functional Responsibility

- Finance
- General Management
- Human Resources
- Legal/Security
- Marketing
- Operations
- Other
- Quality/Employee Development
- Sales

2% 9% 4% 7%
18%
7%
49%
2% 2%

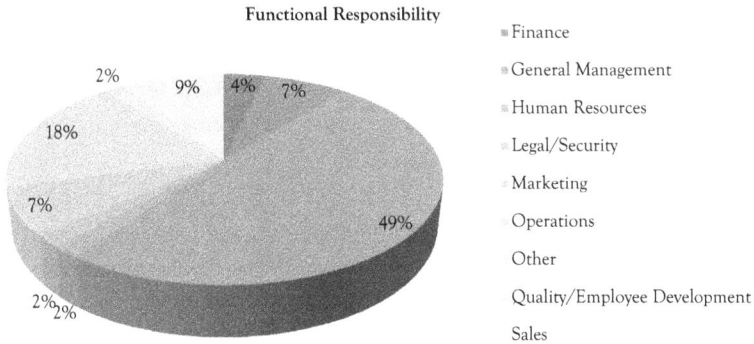

Figure 2.5 Functional responsibility breakdown of respondents

Initial Analysis of Survey Replies

Who Is a Best Boss?

While no two Best Bosses could be described with an identical constellation of traits or personal characteristics, each brought a collection of personal attributes that served to foster a bond between the employee and said boss. Approximately 90 traits were mentioned by respondents, and they fall into the categories outlined in Table 2.1.

Among all these, we identified nearly a dozen traits (presented in Figure 2.6), which were mentioned most frequently to describe a Best Boss.

In our view, the aforementioned qualities are *traits*, that is, characteristics of a person that are either inherent (e.g., "bright") or are developed over a lifetime (e.g., "fair and ethical"). What was most interesting about this collection, however, was the way in which certain traits were balanced by other traits. For example, while a Best Boss was frequently

Table 2.1 Categories of traits most frequently mentioned in describing best boss personal characteristics

Category	Percentage (%)
Types of relationships	42
Leadership style	18
Integrity	15
Outlook	14
Intellectual abilities	11

Bright – very smart	Thoughtful and thorough	Fair and ethical	Respectful
Humble, unassuming and authentic	Positive, optimistic, "can do" attitude	Demonstrates a sense of humor; fun	Accessible and supportive

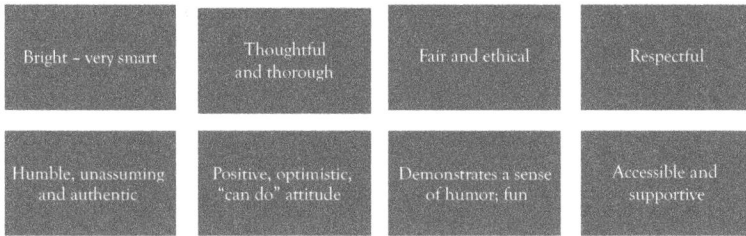

Figure 2.6 Traits most frequently mentioned in describing best boss personal characteristics

described as bright, he or she was also described as being humble and unassuming—not arrogant, as those in power can sometimes be. Another example is the idea of a boss being thorough, without being critical or micro-managing. Instead, the Best Boss seems to come from a place of positivity and empowerment.

Dimensions of Behavior: What Does a Best Boss Do?

We were fortunate to receive hundreds of behavior descriptions of specific Best Boss behavior and impact. To begin, a first pass was made through all of these statements to identify major categories of behavior which could potentially be used to organize and better understand the Best Boss relationship. A total of five categories were identified, what we call "dimensions." Next, a second, more detailed review was made by two raters (i.e., two of the authors) of all behavior descriptions. They independently placed each discrete behavior description into one of the five identified categories. Finally, another rater (i.e., the third author) then independently verified agreement with this placement. Behavior descriptions that did not achieve 100 percent agreement of category placement were dropped from the analysis.

In conclusion, our content analysis of survey replies identified the following five categories or dimensions of behavior indicating that a Best Boss:

- Has a *higher purpose* beyond self-profit or self-interest;
- Observes, acknowledges, and *activates* present and future *potential* of direct reports;

- Freely and regularly imparts business acumen, knowledge and expectations, and then *promotes dynamic autonomy;*
- Provides *pervasive*, multidimensional *feedback*; and
- Inspires continuous learning.

While we acknowledged the robustness and integrity of these categories, we collectively observed they did not reveal anything particularly groundbreaking. For example, it is not news that values-driven leaders are appreciated by those they lead and manage, or that comprehensive feedback benefits employee–boss relationships when that feedback is provided skillfully. Certainly, leaders are expected to help their employees develop and grow. Nor did these dimensions begin to capture the essence of how a Best Boss and direct report relate to one another in the workplace. To get at this, we returned to our database to study the repertoire of behaviors within a single survey participant's response, and from there, discovered something both interesting and new. Our value-added learnings and insights with respect to the employee–boss relationship, as well as the impact of organizational and external economic factors on Best Boss behavior, are presented in the chapters that follow.

CHAPTER 3

The Best Boss Leadership Approach

The approach of a Best Boss seems to embody three distinct features:

1. A trusting relationship between self and direct report;
2. A virtuous (i.e., positively reinforcing) system of deliberate and focused interaction between self and direct report that accounts for the growing trust; and
3. A favorable cycle of performance that unfolds between Best Boss and direct report that is born out of the first two features.

In short, the Best Boss approach is represented by a virtuous system of interaction that leads to a virtuous cycle of performance. Allow us to explain.

A Relationship Based on Trust and Mutual Respect

We hypothesize that there is a virtuous system of interaction between a Best Boss and direct report, and that "relationship" lies at the heart of it. The relationship develops because the direct report understands the behaviors, traits, and demeanor of the Best Boss (typically a person with formal organizational power) convey positive intent, and that intent is focused directly on the individual. To put it simply, trust is established between the Best Boss and direct report.

> He was always willing to support me. Regardless of the situation, he had my back.

> Most of all, I always felt that he had my back. Joe celebrated my successes, always making me feel like the one being celebrated and he shared responsibility for any setbacks. Truly a gem!

He helped me to retain my sense of 'self' and to stay calm and productive in a highly stressful environment. He made me feel trusted.

More specifically, it is through positive interactions across robust dimensions—ones that are highly relevant to both employee and boss—that trust develops. To get a sense of how we arrived at this, it is revealing to look across an individual participant's responses to the entire survey, versus looking across participants for responses to an individual survey question. Below, in Table 3.1, is a single study participant's verbatim quotes, presented within the context of our defined dimensions and derived from the entire, completed survey. In this case, a VP level employee describes their executive boss, "Joe." From this type of analysis, we can imagine how a trusting relationship forms over time: One can observe the employee's perception of a positive or virtuous intent to underpin each dimension.

There were other notable observations about relationship we were able to discern. First, not every Best Boss will connect with every direct report—in other words, the relationship appears to depend on both the boss and the employee. We had firsthand evidence of this when author Duncan was able to confirm that he had also worked with Joe, and that while he was a good boss, never did Duncan consider Joe one of his Best Bosses! Furthermore, we noticed relationship took on a variety of forms, since not every Best Boss

Table 3.1 *A single participant's verbatim responses to the Best Boss survey*

Leads from a Higher Purpose	Activates Potential	Promotes Dynamic Autonomy	Provides Pervasive Feedback	Inspires Continuous Learning
"He made me believe that you could lead with your heart as well as your wisdom, that competence and firmness need not be at odds with compassion and integrity."	"He believed in me and trusted me to lead. My competence was a given in his mind."	"He gave me room to lead my own organization, but was always available if I needed him."	"He helped me feel more confident when I was reaching beyond my comfort zone, and was an honest mirror when I needed to see how others were perceiving me."	"He believed that mistakes were fine if you identified them quickly, owned them, and learned from them."

described in the study was actually a boss. Some people chose to write about a former coach or teacher, where another chose to write about a very senior leader—an indirect boss. From this angle, we described relationship in a variety of ways; for example, the trusting relationship could be described as collegial, mentoring, coaching, personal, etc. Despite these differences, the common thread in the survey replies suggests a trust that developed between the individual and the boss, which grew out of the behaviors, traits, and overall demeanor of the Best Boss.

A "Synergistic and Virtuous System" of Interaction

A closer look at the five dimensions reveals that in addition to positive intent, there is a natural synergy among them. In other words, the interaction of these components produces a total effect greater than the sum of the individual elements. Theoretically, it makes sense that "Leads from a Higher Purpose," "Promotes Dynamic Autonomy," and "Provides Pervasive Feedback" work together. For example, a Best Boss would be remiss to "promote autonomy" without providing regular feedback to a direct report in order to reinforce and reward progress and to redirect effort as needed. With regular feedback, learning and individual growth are likely occurring, and from this, an employee might conclude that the boss is truly focused on something other than the boss' own self-interest, which suggests a higher purpose.

We also believe that synergy develops between the boss and the employee based on the content of their interactions (i.e., the behavioral domains represented in the dimensions, to be discussed in further detail in forthcoming chapters) and the skill and overall demeanor with which the Best Boss relates to the employee. To wrap our arms around this, we initially envisioned a simple reinforcing loop as depicted in Figure 3.1.

Our initial view of the creation of synergy between dimensions included the following:

- Boss who leads from a higher purpose, meaning that she or he leads for more than self-interest, activates employee potential by simply acknowledging an employee's background and experience, and thus provides an opportunity for the employee to contribute a perspective on an important issue.

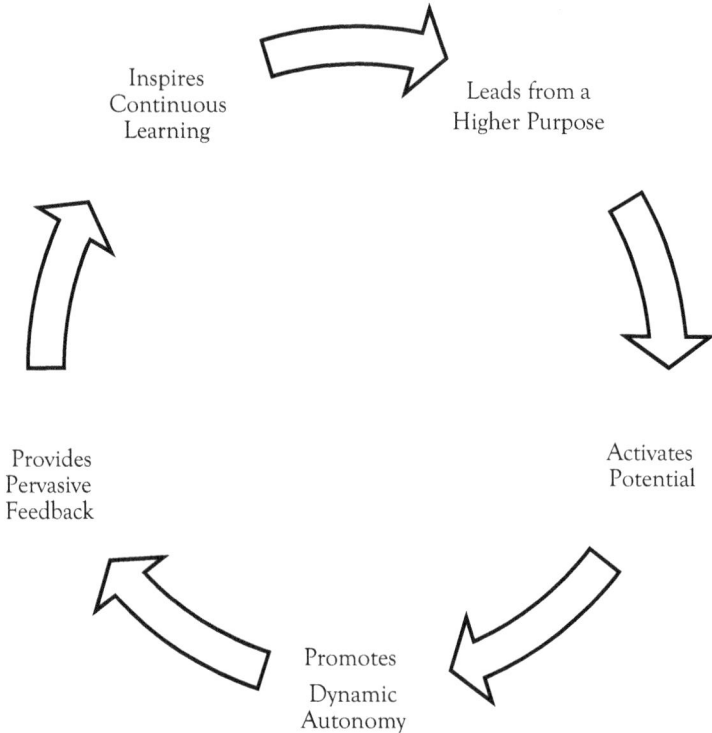

Figure 3.1 Best boss "system" as a single reinforcing loop

- Employee is attentive now. Engaged!
- Boss continues to capture employee attention by sharing wisdom, knowledge, and clear expectations for performance; now gives the employee "space" to perform.
- Boss is invested in employee success, so he or she provides continual feedback to help employee grow, develop, and achieve goals.
- Boss informs the growing relationship by saying, "I know you will make mistakes, just don't keep them from me. We will learn from them and fix them together."

Trust continues. Relationships grow and higher purpose is achieved for the Best Boss as the employee learns, develops, and achieves real results.

As we continued to review the data, we quickly realized there were likely limitless ways for a Best Boss and direct report to connect, as shown in Figure 3.2.

This conceptualization raised questions:

- What if we were to think of the Best Boss traits and behavioral domains as the apparent boundaries for interaction?
- What if it is *not* necessarily an orderly progression from one dimension to the next, but one that pivots and ricochets off of one dimension to another as boss and direct report interact in ways that build trust and meaningful connection over time?
- In other words, we suspect that by continually directing attention toward two or more of these five areas, a Best Boss can bring about a unique, generative, and rewarding relationship with their direct report based on trust and respect, which essentially entertains the interests of employee, the boss, and ultimately the organization.

We looked at our theory in relationship to the response frequencies for the five dimensions, as shown in Figure 3.3. By far, the most

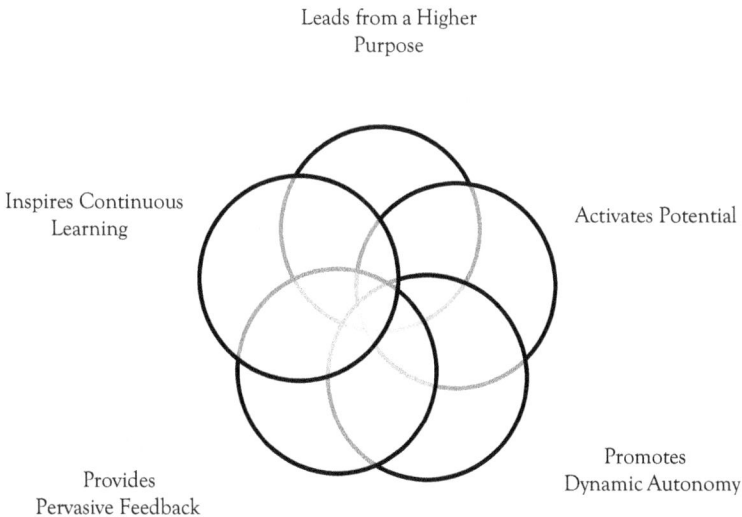

Figure 3.2 Best boss synergistic system of interaction

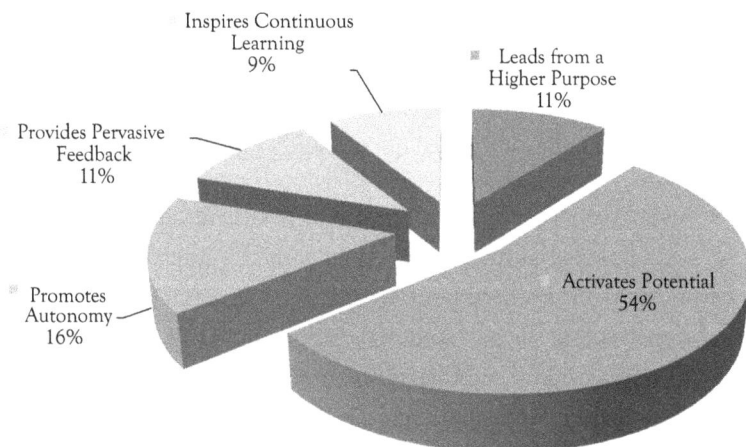

Figure 3.3 Response frequencies for the five dimensions of the best boss model

frequently reported dimension was Activates Potential, with 54 percent of respondents suggesting their Best Boss was focused on their professional development and success at work. On the other hand, study participants reported the other dimensions between 9 and 16 percent of the time.

Why might Activates Potential be identified as a distinguishing feature of a Best Boss? Perhaps it is due to the notable effect that a boss' positive attention on an employee's growth and success can have on not only his or her work satisfaction, but also their life satisfaction. Everything is different when your boss has your professional best interests front and center, and as an employee—you know it! For the moment, put yourself in the employee's shoes. Bosses exert a lot of power over their employees and a boss has significant impact on the employee's ability:

- To derive intrinsic motivation through work, based on assignments, opportunities, and experiences offered by the boss;
- To be held in regard by other leaders, based on how the boss presents the employee to peers and higher-level leaders; and
- To stay employed and be rewarded based on performance appraisals, which of course are of monumental importance to the individual in order to meet basic human needs for self, and potentially others.

These are true attention-getters, particularly in the context of a boss who is focused on activating an employee's potential.

Rather than conclude, however, that Activates Potential is the most important dimension, we are drawn to the realization that it is the *interaction* of the dimensions that is key. To argue by analogy, is it appropriate to identify the nervous system, the circulatory system, the digestive system, or any other internal system as the most important in the successful functioning of the human body? Obviously not, as it is the successful interdependence_of these systems that yields a healthy, functioning body overall. We believe the same sort of interdependency exists between and among the five Best Boss dimensions we have identified. And, because of the positivity that underpins all dimensions, trust, and meaningful connection between the Best Boss and employee are reinforced over and over again. Study participants said as much.

To demonstrate this point, see Table 3.2 to consider the resulting impact on an employee's ability to trust and meaningfully relate to the boss when comparing a boss' neutral or negative orientation to a positive one in the areas of purpose, feedback, autonomy, and learning.

A Virtuous Cycle of Performance

Is the impact of a Best Boss sustainable? Old habits and unproductive ways of behaving can be hard to change, not only for employees, but for those trying to become better leaders as well. There is a human tendency to regress back to old, less effective ways. In the relationship between a Best Boss and direct report, we observe dynamics that work against this gravitational pull: We propose that the synergistic and virtuous system of interaction becomes self-reinforcing over time, and leads to a virtuous cycle of performance as mutually beneficial impacts become realized. In other words:

- The employee may become more engaged by working on projects of interest that grow skills and knowledge;
- The boss observes high levels of performance and is gratified to observe individual growth in the direct report; and
- Goals are achieved and performance is recognized and/or rewarded by the organization for both employee and boss, increasing the probability of success in future endeavors involving boss and employee.

Table 3.2 The importance of boss' attention in leading direct reports

Dimensions (Traditional Areas of Focus)	Nature of Boss Attention	
	Neutral or Negative	Positive or Virtuous
	Common Employee Response (based on experience with the boss or through "default" interpretation in the absence of the boss' deliberate philosophy and/or behavior)	Employee Response in Best Boss Study (based on Best Boss deliberate philosophy and/or behavior)
Purpose	Employee may feel like a tool toward the purpose of "maximizing shareholder profits"	Employee feels his or her interests are incorporated into the interests of the boss and organization "He gave me the confidence I needed to make a huge career change. He also supported me instead of maximizing his self-interests (by keeping me there). He relieved me of the obligation I felt to stay loyal to the company and to him. I felt confident, freed, and respected."
Feedback	Employee may feel put down, defensive, paranoid, demoralized	Employee feels supported, motivated, engaged "He would give praise where appropriate and give direct feedback when needed. He would share with me things I did well and offer advice when things didn't go as well. He wasn't condescending about it, just helpful … even when he was stressed to the max"
Autonomy	Employee may feel micromanaged versus trusted to act autonomously	Employee can show what he or she knows, trusting that the "dynamic" support of the boss exists "[He] had the uncanny ability to summarize a major corporate challenge on one piece of paper and then explain. He brought out the best in others and did not lose a sense of humor under pressure. Working for [him] helped me see the corporate world through the eyes of the CEO. He taught people to apply principle and mission assessment before analytics."
Learning	Employee may feel shame for mistake; strives to "not rock the boat"	Employee feels safe to learn through both mistakes and successes "He always had my back, but if I made a mistake, he would come to me and discuss 'other options.' I never felt like a failure. Mistakes were seen as part of the growth process in a person's life"

This line of reasoning is conceptually related to some of the impacts identified by those direct reports in the study, as shown in Table 3.3 below. We will take a broader and deeper look into impact in Chapter 11, Why Best Bosses Matter.

Trust is at the foundation of the relationship between a Best Boss and direct report. It begins when the employee realizes that through both character and behavior, the Best Boss fundamentally "has his/her back" in key areas as suggested by the dimensions we identified. Over time, as the relationship grows, a virtuous cycle of performance unfolds. This dynamic often carries forward into future relationships as a leadership legacy, when the direct report moves into a leadership position. Employee, boss, and organization all win as a result of the Best Boss Leadership Approach.

Table 3.3 Direct report impacts identified in the Best Boss study

Impact On...	Respondent Statistics
Individual Performance	93 percent said that their performance excelled while working for their Best Boss
Level of Engagement	82 percent made statements or used terms that indicated high engagement
Development and Career	77 percent said that their Best Boss had a positive impact on both their personal development and career development
Ability to Lead	36 percent made a direct statement on how they became better leaders because of the Best Boss relationship
Personhood	24 percent made a direct statement on how their Best Boss made them a better person

CHAPTER 4

Leads From a Higher Purpose

Definition

The Best Boss demonstrates a purpose beyond self and/or organizational interests by taking positive action on behalf of the direct report through an authentic relationship.

Favorite Quotes From the Study

He gave me the confidence I needed to make a huge career change. He also supported *me* instead of maximizing his self-interests (by keeping me there). He relieved me of the obligation I felt to stay loyal to the company and to him.

He just took that extra step ... a personal step, a human step and always in a most genuine way.

He made you want to be a better person.

Discussion

Simply put, there seems to be a purpose beyond self-profit or organizational interest inherent in the motivations and behaviors of the Best Boss—a conscious or subconscious consideration of why he or she does what he or she does, day in and day out. What is missing from the repertoire of the Best Boss is an obsession with achieving results to the exclusion of anything humane. Most definitely, the Best Boss is focused on achieving results and high levels of performance, but so is he or she focused on considerations of how results are obtained (e.g., values or ethics-based) as reflected in the following study quotes:

> Saw my gifts and moved me into positions that fit my gifts ... in a sense he was an advocate for my best self.

> The trust and respect were a function of common values that we shared which provided the foundation for a chemistry in 'how' we operated ... inclusive but beyond just 'what' we needed to accomplish... He made me believe that you could lead with your heart as well as your wisdom, that competence and firmness need not be at odds with compassion and integrity.

> My favorite was, when facing a particularly difficult decision, his first question was always 'What is the right thing to do?' This is where all conversations started and we worked toward a solution from there.

Higher purpose also seemed to manifest in the Best Boss' interest in the holistic growth and development of the employee. In this regard, an employee was viewed as more than someone who just performed the job, but also as a person whose life extended beyond work in myriad ways.

> Far more importantly, you made me a better wife, mother, daughter, and friend by sharing your contagious love of life. You taught me to take chances, celebrate success, and appreciate that if I don't make mistakes, I'm not challenging myself enough.

> He let me in on small bits of his personal life- not too much, but enough to let me know him as a person. He made jokes. He sent me funny things that he knew my husband would like for me to share at home.

> Later that afternoon, he called to see how my mom was doing. He just took that extra step.... again, in a most genuine way.

Additionally, the time Don takes to talk with me about how I'm doing, both personally and professionally, makes me feel like he really cares about me as a person and is invested in me as an employee.

While no one in our study referred to his or her Best Boss as having a "higher purpose," it was easy for us to identify this dimension based on these and other comments and stories. In addition, nowhere in our study did anyone make explicit that higher purpose was a deliberate part of their Best Boss' leadership style. We speculate that for some leaders, demonstration of higher purpose is a conscious effort, and for others it may be unconscious—deeply embedded in an individual's modus operandi, perhaps stemming from family values, religious and/or cultural beliefs, and so on.

Igniting the System

Having a higher purpose is focused on the human aspects of leadership, such as having the intention to help others grow and achieving results in moral, value-based ways. This dimension aligns with the other four dimensions of the Best Boss model, and such alignment precludes employee cynicism that often arises when they perceive their leader to espouse certain values without behaving in accordance to them, or without integrating them into organizational practices and processes. Here are several examples with corresponding quotes from our study that lend credence to our hypothesis on the Best Boss approach to leading.

Activates Potential

Leading from a higher purpose, the Best Boss is drawn to align employee developmental needs and/or talents to the requirements of the work, simultaneously:

(From Courtney's late reply to study):

He highly valued my thinking, judgment and input and solicited it often in making decisions. This was empowering. He believed in potential and opened doors for me into new experiences, roles, and opportunities. He always had my best interests in mind, and his actions spoke as loudly as his words.

He was my advocate and champion and always made sure that the right people knew who I was and what I could do.

Promotes Dynamic Autonomy

Driven not just by the needs of the organization but also by the developmental needs and interests of the employee, a Best Boss understands the vital importance of sharing knowledge, expertise, and expectations before setting the individual onto a productive, self-directed path.

Mike had a vision of what he wanted to do and what we needed to do and he shared it with me.

He gave me the big picture and let me run things my way.

He had high expectations for me ... told me so ... and then let me run with it. I was as independent as I needed to be .... kept him informed, went to him with questions/issues, and then he just let me go. He helped me develop my resourcefulness (if that is a word), leadership, big picture perspective, etc.

Provides Pervasive Feedback

A Best Boss with higher purpose understands the necessity of feedback to facilitate, reinforce, or redirect performance and how consequential it is for the employee to receive it, if in fact the employee is a true focus of interest.

He was very direct in his feedback and would force me to look my self-doubt in the eye and deal with it.

He would give praise where appropriate and give direct feedback when needed. He would share with me things I did well and offer advice when things didn't go as well. He wasn't condescending about it, just helpful ... even when he was stressed to the max.

He was an honest mirror when I needed to see how others were perceiving me.

Inspires Continuous Learning

The Best Boss acknowledges the inevitability of an employee making mistakes and reframes the mistake in a positive, supportive way that leads to identifying root causes and promotes learning. In turn, we can hypothesize, based on reported study impacts, that the learning is applied forward, advancing individual growth and furthering company goals.

You allowed me to fail and not crucify me ... what a gift.

He had an ability to help me and others extract all that could be learned from a given opportunity.

Related Thinking

There are countless books and articles on the topic of values-based leadership—the idea that leaders can draw on the values of the organization, as well as their own, to meaningfully shape their interactions with direct reports. There are even programs offered in which executives can earn advanced degrees in values-driven leadership, as is the case at the Center for Values-Driven Leadership at Benedictine University in Lisle, Illinois. Here, doctoral candidates proceed through curricula emphasizing not only short- and long-term company value, but also focus on enhancing the lives of people, society, and the sustainability of the planet.

One of the most famous works that speaks to the themes drawn from our study on higher purpose comes from Robert Greenleaf:

The servant-leader is servant first ... It begins with the natural feeling that one wants to serve, to serve first. Then conscious choice brings one to aspire to lead ...The best test, and difficult to administer is:

do those served grow as persons: do they, while being served, become healthier, wiser, freer, more autonomous, more likely themselves to become servants? (Greenleaf 1970, p. 15).

Furthermore, "Commitment to the Growth of People" is one of the 10 defining characteristic of a servant leader as described by Larry Spears, President and CEO of the Larry C. Spears Center for Servant-Leadership, Inc.:

> Servant-leaders believe that people have an intrinsic value beyond their tangible contributions as workers. As such, the servant-leader is deeply committed to the growth of each and every individual within his or her organization. The servant-leader recognizes the tremendous responsibility to do everything in his or her power to nurture the personal and professional growth of employees and colleagues. (Spears 2010, 29)

We can find more connections to this Best Boss dimension by recalling notable business leaders from the past. While controversy surrounds his leadership legacy, the late former CEO of General Electric, Jack Welch, felt strongly about managing tension between the company's values and the desire to achieve financial results. He was very vocal about four types of leaders that he described by virtue of a two-by-two matrix, with results along one dimension and GE's values along the other. This matrix produced the four types of leaders and the company's perspective on retaining each type:

- Type I: A highly valued leader who shares GE's values and achieves financial targets (stay)
- Type II: Neither achieves financial targets nor shares company values (leave)
- Type III: Shares company values but misses financial targets (given another chance or two)
- Type IV: Does not share GE values but achieves financial targets (remove)

In GE's 2000 Annual Report, Welch provided a compelling reason for removing Type IV leaders:

> …Type IV is… the "go-to" manager, the hammer, who delivers the bacon but does it on the backs of people, often 'kissing up and kicking down' during the process. This type is the toughest to part with because organizations always want to deliver—it's in the blood— and to let someone go who gets the job done is yet another unnatural act. But we have to remove these Type IVs because they have the power, by themselves, to destroy the open, informal, trust-based culture we need to win today and tomorrow. (2000 GE Annual Report, p. 5).

There is incredible value for employees, leaders, companies, and society as a whole when managers incorporate higher purpose into the way they lead. This may be particularly true for Millennials, who seek employment within organizations that exude purpose in tangible ways. How might life be different with Best Bosses who lead from a higher purpose? Take a moment to imagine: Employees feel valued and return the sentiment in the ways they perform, with benefit to the organization. Mindful managers feel the intrinsic reward of leading well. The positivity—such as engagement, equanimity, organizational success—realized by all of the preceding feeds into society with systemic impact, translating to company growth, job creation, discretionary income for spending, donations to not-for-profit organizations, and more.

Author Experience With Higher Purpose

From Toni

Toni can think of a good story that describes an excellent manager who may never have considered whether or not he leads with a higher purpose. But indeed, he does. This excellent people leader described an employee in his organization who was slated for termination. Despite exceptional analytical and computer skills, no manager wanted to absorb this person into his or her department due to limitations in interpersonal skill and emotional competence. Nonetheless, this particular leader offered to bring the employee into his organization. Herein lies a higher purpose, enacted on the part of a vulnerable other.

The leader began their boss–employee relationship by candidly and compassionately delivering the difficult feedback that was essential for this person to hear, in addition to his important and admirable strengths. Then, the leader made clear what would be expected for this individual to be successful in his new role, taking time to provide concrete examples of acceptable and unacceptable behaviors, as well as describing the department culture. As a result, the employee was receptive to ongoing coaching from the boss, and over time, shifted his behavior and ultimately thrived in this new role for many years. His relationship with the leader exists to this day.

Immediate Implications for the Workplace

Stories like this make us wonder how many employees have been cast aside for lack of manager will, and undoubtedly, lack of skill in undertaking the more demanding path of managing employee behavior and/or performance. It is all too easy to understand the stress and strain this deficit heaps onto the terminated employee. It is also worth considering, however, what is lost to an organization that engages in numerous terminations of those who would ultimately benefit the organization because of leaders who do not understand why, when, or how to intervene on behalf of struggling or disengaged employee.

There is much to be gained from managers who exude a higher purpose in the way they lead. Quite frankly, it doesn't even require large investments in training and development in order to bring this about. Since it always begins at the top, CEOs can set the tone of leadership through their own words and actions—which are regularly and prominently shared—and astute leaders will take note and follow suit. The organization as a whole will begin to align itself in this way, making it much easier for those individuals who naturally lead this way.

CEOs can also establish a Leadership Philosophy that spells out a higher purpose in leading employees, which every people leader within the organization can abide by. To illuminate this point, we would like to share a few excerpts from an interview with an amazing leader: Peggy Troy, CEO of Children's, the pediatric hospital in Milwaukee:

What always grounds us is purpose. We are here to serve, and we must have servant leaders on our team. People need to trust you as a leader and believe that you are always going to be honest and forthright. You can't lead with ego; you have to lead with humility.

Following our interview with Peggy, we had the opportunity to discuss her leadership philosophy and approach—developed while working for her Best Boss, Gary Shorb, CEO of Children's Hospital of Memphis—with three of her direct reports, who all acknowledged Peggy as their Best Boss, too. Specific to purpose, Laura Miller, former VP of Planning for the hospital, provided an example of how Peggy sets the tone for all people managers to lead with a higher purpose:

> She speaks to every employee. It could be someone on the senior team, it could be a nurse on the floor or a housekeeper; she wants them to know who she is, she wants to express kindness. Maybe most importantly, she wants to hear from them and will ask them, "how is it going, what do you need?"

We will share a bit more from Peggy Troy and her team later in the book when we discuss Best Bosses and leadership legacy. To watch a video of these interviews with Peggy and her team, please follow the link below and scroll down to the embedded video: https://vantageleadership.com/leaders/best-boss-experience/

As a final consideration, a formal philosophy of leadership can be articulated into behaviors that are, in turn, incorporated into performance appraisals of managers who lead people. Measuring performance in this way and aligning performance outcomes with reward systems will not only make expectations clear, but will also promote a culture of Best Boss leadership over time.

Self-Reflection

Now that you have read and thought about the dimension of higher purpose in leadership, take a moment and reflect on the extent to which you demonstrate this dimension's related behaviors.

I.	Leads from a Higher Purpose (On a 5-point extent of use scale: To what extent do you typically...)				
	Not at All	To a Small Extent	To Some Extent	To a Moderate Extent	To a Large Extent
	1	2	3	4	5

Instructions: Using the scale above, write the number in the space to the left of each survey item that best represents your current use of the behavior. Next, calculate the average score and fill in the result in the space provided. At your option, you may use this information in Chapter 9, How to Become a Better Boss.

	Take the "extra step" to reach out to direct reports in a genuine way
	Work to get to know direct reports personally, not just as employees
	Show direct reports that high performance expectations are consistent with compassion
	Demonstrate a strong "moral compass" in your work
	Set your self-interest aside when helping direct reports grow in their careers
	Demonstrate a purpose in your work that goes beyond simply making money
	Care for people in their lives, not just for what they can do for you on the job
	Exhibit shared values in your relationship with direct reports
	Encourage direct reports to do what is ethical when faced with a difficult decision
	Stand by your direct reports in practically every circumstance
(fill in average)	Average Extent of Use: Leads from a Higher Purpose

CHAPTER 5

Activates Potential

Definition

The Best Boss observes, values, acknowledges, and takes steps to activate the present capability and future potential of the individual.

Favorite Quotes From the Study

Worked hard to provide a leadership role for me in those events and would often defer to or ask my opinion in front of his very important customers. This was a gesture of explicit trust and belief in what I could bring to the table and it gave me just enough runway over time to develop confidence among a very select and successful group of people.

He would do all sorts of things to get me out of my comfort zone—push me, even sometimes provoke me. He saw the potential but also saw that I was holding something back and wouldn't accept that I was giving everything I had to give.

[Because of my Best Boss] I was soaring on the learning curve. Decades later, I understood that the content of my work (and the team at our location) was light years ahead of my peers.

He showed me at such an early phase in my career that you should have an expectation to learn and develop in any job. I know he created more opportunities for me than most managers, but I also took full advantage of each one and I believe that is because I felt like I earned them, but they were not given without an expectation that I do something of value with what I learned.

Discussion

Leaders should, and indeed are, often expected to develop the skills and competencies of their people. So, as we analyzed our survey data, it was not a surprise to see development as the most mentioned of the five leadership dimensions. Yet, as we dug deeper, it became clear from our analysis that this dimension was far more robust than we initially imagined. Our study showed that Best Bosses *activate potential* by instinctively assuming that everyone has unique capabilities. These leaders not only identify potential but also make it their mission to help the individual personally discover it, and then bring that potential to life in any way possible.

Both the Best Boss and direct report play separate yet equal roles if potential is to be successfully unleashed. Often it starts with a simple acknowledgement of respect toward the individual. As a bond based on mutual respect and trust develops, the Best Boss seeks opportunities to expose an individual to a variety of experiences that allows them to learn and grow. The Best Boss nurtures development with both constructive criticism and recognition to ensure learning lessons are being comprehended. And, perhaps most important of all, the Best Boss positively and consistently encourages the individual through every success *and* failure.

But this is only half of the activating potential process. The individual must take a risk, often by overcoming fear, uncertainty, or inertia, to advance their development. They have to believe in themselves as much as their Best Boss does. And, perhaps most importantly, they need to trust that their Best Boss will always support them, no matter the result.

Best Bosses exhibit four specific traits that help awaken potential. They are consistently challenging, supportive, trusting, and advocating in their leadership of others. The following survey quotes illustrate these traits:

I feel that George was not only advocating for me but kept pushing me to get better and better.

Because of her support, I feel more confident in my skills and in the work I accomplish. I also feel better prepared to handle challenging assignments and perform work that may be outside of my comfort zone.

His encouragement and trust in me caused me to go above and beyond the expectations of the job. For that reason, I grew in ways that I never expected. My work was often difficult but always left me feeling accomplished and good about what I was doing.

My Best Boss saw my gifts and moved me into positions that fit my gifts … in a sense, he was an advocate for my best self.

While activating potential presents itself in an individual's performance and engagement, the long-term return on the activating potential investment can have positive implications that can last well into one's career. Call it the cumulative effect of discovering a capability that pays dividends throughout a working life.

I would tell my (Best Boss) that he had a profound effect on me and helped to shape me as a professional, as a leader, as a contributor, and as a teammate. The experience of working with him, literally, changed the course of my career and helped me understand how to pull the best out of myself and others.

Igniting the System

It is difficult to discover and then activate your potential on your own. It takes a village of people from your life—friends, parents, school counselors, teachers, coaches, mentors, and more to help you recognize the individual gifts you possess. Often, one of the most important people in your village is a great boss who intuitively understands how to behave across the other dimensions to unleash one's potential. Below, we take a look at the other four Best Boss Leadership dimensions, and how they interact with the "Activates Potential" dimension.

Leads From a Higher Purpose

Placing the needs of the individual above, or at least on par, with the business needs of the organization is a critical element in accelerating the development of an individual so that they can more fully contribute today *and* tomorrow.

How much he influenced my life professionally! I would do whatever he asked me to do—no questions asked because he could be trusted, and I knew he would never ask me to do anything that would harm my career or me.

Promotes Dynamic Autonomy

Discovering and realizing one's potential requires the freedom to make autonomous decisions once a foundation of expertise, organizational knowledge, and clear expectations is provided.

> My Best Boss worked hard to provide a leadership role for me in those events and would often defer to or ask my opinion in front of his very important customers. This was a gesture of explicit trust and belief in what I could bring to the table. and it gave me just enough runway over time to develop confidence.

Provides Pervasive Feedback

For the individual to understand how potential successfully develops into capability and performance, it is mandatory to provide both respectful constructive criticism and positive reinforcement.

> He helped me feel more confident when I was reaching beyond my comfort zone, and he was an honest mirror when I needed to see how others were perceiving me. Most of all, I always felt that he had my back.

Inspires Continuous Learning

Learning, growth, and development are accelerated by encouraging progressive risk-taking in concert with an individual's perceived talents and aspirations, especially when the person anticipates support instead of fearing reprisal.

I believe she also showed me at such an early phase in my career that work could be fun and that you should have an expectation to learn and develop in any job. I know she created more opportunities for me than most managers and I took full advantage of each one. But they were not given without an expectation that I do something of value with what I learned.

Related Thinking

In her book *Mindset: The New Psychology of Success*, Dr. Carol Dweck identifies two mindsets that people can have about their talents and abilities. Those with a fixed mindset believe that their talents and abilities are static and unchangeable. People with a growth mindset, on the other hand, think of talents and abilities as things that can develop through teaching, effort, and practice. In the growth mindset, talent is something you build upon and develop, not something you simply accept and utilize in an unchanged form. Dweck's research shows that a growth mindset can elicit better performance by inducing a healthy attitude toward practice and learning, seeking feedback, and developing resilience to setbacks (Dweck 2016).

We contend that a Best Boss behaves in a way that cultivates and reinforces a growth mindset in his or her own direct reports. This begins with a focus on observing and acknowledging a person's given talents and skills. Realization of potential continues with opportunities to execute one's skills while receiving continuous feedback, support, and a welcome dissection of mistakes made—all provided through the philosophy and behavior of a Best Boss.

Author Experience With Activates Potential

From Duncan

I had just been promoted to a new role, Labor Relations Representative, in a large manufacturing plant—and I was nervous. While any transition can be unsettling, this one had me concerned. I had no labor relations experience, did not enjoy conflict, and, having a "baby face" made me look much younger than my 28 years of age. I worried that the union reps, who I would be dealing with on a day-to-day basis, would eat me alive. Admittedly, this was not my dream job, but it was back in the day when the corporation managed your career the way they saw fit, and you were just along for the ride.

When I arrived at the facility, my new boss, Ed, invited me into his office to chat. Shortly after we sat down, we were notified that the union president, Rudy, was in the lobby and wanted to meet with him. Just hearing the name Rudy scared me. Union presidents are never named Brett or Zach. If they were, it would not be so intimidating. A few minutes later, Rudy enters Ed's office, walks right past where I was sitting, and takes a seat directly in front of Ed. There was no acknowledgement of my presence. His main concern seemed to be a white Styrofoam cup he was holding in his right hand. After spitting tobacco juice into the cup, Rudy pointed at me and asked, "Who's Mr. Shiny Pants?" I immediately started questioning every decision I had ever made in my life that brought me to this moment in time. Should I just quit? How would I survive?

One of the main parts of my job was investigating grievances that could not be settled between the foremen and union rep. Most grievances involved disputes about overtime, work rules, and the like. The most contentious situations involved employees who were discharged. Twice per month, our Vice President of HR, Joe, my boss, Ed, and I would meet with the union reps to discuss and attempt to settle the grievances at what was called an Agenda meeting. Those grievances that remained unsettled were usually arbitrated at a later date. I attended my first Agenda meeting during my second week on the job and, since I was new, I did not do much outside of taking notes. The combative nature of the meeting was not lost on me.

Two weeks later, Ed, Joe and I met to prepare for the next Agenda meeting. As we discussed the grievances, Joe looked at his calendar and said, "I will be travelling on business and won't be at the next Agenda meeting." Ed checked his calendar and reminded Joe that he was travelling with him. Joe looked at me and said, "Well, I guess you're up." I waited for a chuckle because I figured he was kidding. There was not a chance he would let me run the Agenda meeting. I was green… a rookie… totally not ready for this responsibility. The union would slaughter me! Much to my chagrin, he was completely serious.

The day of the Agenda meeting arrived. After a night of about 20 minutes' worth of sleep, I drove into the plant and went to the meeting room early. My first quandary was where I should sit. The conference room table was oblong with about 14 chairs sitting around it. There was one chair at each end where Joe and Rudy sat. But there was no Joe or Ed at this meeting. Just me. I decided to sit in Joe's chair, which is where I was sitting when the union committee arrived. The first one to enter the room was, of course, Rudy, with Styrofoam cup obediently in his hand. He asked, "Where is Joe?" "Not here," I replied. "What about Ed?" "With Joe," I said. Then Rudy calls out to the committee, "Come on in boys, fresh meat today." I would like to say the meeting went well, but the truth is, the union had a field day with this rookie.

After such a torturous beginning, I found my rhythm on the job. By the time I left the assignment, I had built strong relationships with everyone on the union committee, including Rudy. We even went golfing a couple times! Joe and Ed's tutelage (and later, Henry's and Jack's) continued throughout my assignment, and they continued to place me in situations that accelerated my development. I argued termination cases before an arbitrator, I met with union leaders to settle contentious grievances before they reached the Agenda meeting, and they encouraged me to share my opinions during contract negotiations. As I reflect on this moment in my career, I realize how much I grew, both as a professional and a person during my time with Joe and Ed. I learned how to build strong interpersonal relationships, manage conflict, and make tough decisions. It all started when Joe and Ed showed their faith in me by pushing me out of my comfort zone and sending me into a battle for which I felt underprepared. Years later I ran into Joe and recounted this experience. I said, "you really threw me to the wolves that day." He just laughed and told me, "I didn't give you anything you couldn't handle, you just needed to learn that you could do it."

Immediate Implications for the Workplace

There used to be an implied contract between you and your employer. You gave them your loyalty and your efforts, and in return the company provided security, benefits, and often, career longevity. A durable connection existed between the individual and organization. It was not perfect, but it was how the world worked, and it provided some sense of balance.

Over the past three decades, this contract has disintegrated. The individual employee has felt the fallout of the rapidly evolving workplace. Demands are higher, resources are fewer, technology has made work/life balance a daily challenge, and change is omnipresent. Words like downsizing, rightsizing, restructuring, outsourcing, and redundancy have become commonplace in our work vocabulary. These churning dynamics have transformed all of us, and especially younger generations, to think much differently about work. Long-term loyalty has been replaced by a free-agent mentality, and "one company, one career" is an antiquated notion today wherein multiple companies and multiple careers are much more the norm. Job hopping, which used to be a resume red flag, is now a proactive career planning strategy.

This change in mindset was noted in a *New York Times* article titled "The Shifting Definition of Worker Loyalty:"

> Now many companies cannot or will not hold up their end of the bargain, so why should the employees hold up theirs? Given the opportunity, they'll take their skills and their portable 401(k)'s elsewhere. Younger generations now bring a different view of careers into the workplace. (Korkki 2011).

The quote below from Matt, an early career professional who Duncan mentored after his graduation from college, illuminates this changed viewpoint:

> I don't expect (or even want) to stay with the same company for my entire career so I need to build my portfolio of skills to make me marketable for my next job and company. I want a company that will invest in my learning and growth as a professional. And, in return, I will work as hard as I can.

This comment offers employers a glimpse of what it will take to retain and engage not only young and talented employees, but those of older generations as well. People now bring a transient mentality to the workplace, and investment by employers in their professional growth is mandatory if they are to remain marketable in the working world. Given the new rules governing work and careers, employees won't stay with an employer for the duration of their career as they typically did a generation ago. Employers who do not invest in the development of their employees will risk losing the very talent they will require to remain competitive in the marketplace.

In addition, talented employees will stay longer if they are led by people who excel in activating their potential. Why? First, because Best Bosses naturally focus on employee learning, development, and growth, which will help keep their portfolio of skills and competencies contemporary in an ever-competitive marketplace of talent. It is important here to note that 77 percent of our study respondents indicated their Best Boss played a significant role in helping them develop skills that led to a successful career. Second, and perhaps more importantly, our study shows that Best Bosses build a trusted and personal relationship with their employees, which, by default, often creates a positive connection with their employer. The topic of organizational connection will be explored further in Chapter 11 ("Why Best Bosses Matter").

Lastly and less frequently, we observed that a Best Boss can actually activate potential by suggesting an employee leave the organization if and when the organizational fit is limiting vital development of the individual. In these cases, the benefits to the employee can be life changing:

> He encouraged me to leave our company when I was frustrated with the business. I then left to run a family business for three years, and now I'm starting my own business that resonates with my personal values deeply. I'm very satisfied with these changes.

Self-Reflection

Now that you have had some time to think about the dimension of Activates Potential, take a moment to reflect on the extent to which you activate potential in the way you lead others.

II.	Activates Potential (On a 5-point extent of use scale: To what extent do you typically...)				
	Not at All	To a Small Extent	To Some Extent	To a Moderate Extent	To a Large Extent
	1	2	3	4	5

Instructions: Using the preceding scale, write the number in the space to the left of each survey item that best represents your current use of the behavior. Next, calculate the average score and fill in the result in the space provided. At your option, you may use this information in Chapter 9 ("How to Become a Better Boss").

	Offer direct reports opportunities to show what they can do
	Treat direct reports as individuals with talents to contribute, regardless of job title or pay level
	Serve as an advocate for your direct reports to perform up to their best potential
	Place your direct reports in situations that "showcase" their talents and allow others to recognize their talents
	Supportively "push" your direct reports to achieve outside of their comfort zone
	Encourage your direct reports to bring forth their recommendations and ideas
	Demonstrate that you value your direct reports' views through acting on their ideas
	Identify challenging situations and deploy direct reports to them so as to accelerate their development
	Identify and address organizational barriers that potentially could hinder the development of direct reports
	Identify and address self-imposed barriers that may impede the performance and development of direct reports
(fill in average)	Average Extent of Use: Activates Potential

CHAPTER 6

Promotes Dynamic Autonomy

Definition

The Best Boss imparts organizational knowledge and big picture thinking, establishes clear expectations, and creates an autonomous space for the individual to perform.

Favorite Quotes From the Study

She helped me understand the bigger picture of the business and how that connected to my goals. Then she allowed me the freedom to act and think, giving me a "white piece of paper" to do my job.

He gave me lots of latitude to do my job, but was always available and willing to spend time with me when I needed guidance.

He had the uncanny ability to summarize a major corporate challenge on one piece of paper and then explain. He brought out the best in others and did not lose a sense of humor under pressure. Working for him helped me see the corporate world through the eyes of the CEO. He taught people to apply principle and mission assessment before analytics.

Discussion

In our experience, less successful bosses may ignore, micromanage, or in a number of other ways, have difficulty conveying their expectations of direct reports. They could perhaps be insecure, or preoccupied by their subordinates' potential to outshine them. In sharp contrast, the Best Boss will take steps to assure a foundation of core skills and competencies, strengthen direct reports' insights about the organization and business, convey their expectations clearly, and encourage independent action based upon direct reports' best thinking. In addition, framing an area in which the direct report can act autonomously conveys trust and a belief in the readiness of the individual to chart their own course of action.

We include the term "dynamic" in our title of this dimension. Poring over all our data, we infer a "bias for action" in the expectations of the Best Boss, communicated explicitly or implicitly. Support provided by the Best Boss seemed to be ongoing, driven by a necessity to provide relevant information to the otherwise autonomous direct report. We infer that this support comes in a variety of ways, for example, communication of changes in company direction or performance and related employee expectations, relevant competitor intelligence, or timely feedback, all offered in an effort to create conditions for an employee's optimal performance.

> He gave me lots of latitude to do my job, but was always available and willing to spend time with me when I needed guidance.

Igniting the System

Promoting a dynamic basis for autonomy is clearly related to all other components of the Best Boss process. In the following sections, we elaborate on and use quotes from the study to illustrate our understanding of these connections.

Leads From a Higher Purpose

Time is perhaps the most valuable resource a boss has to offer. Taking the time to develop direct reports' insights in regards to the broader organization and business clearly demonstrates an investment being made in the employee that goes beyond the immediate needs of the boss. Some additional quotes from the study respondents further clarify our point:

> He personified leadership in what he said, how he said it, and how he behaved. He raised my level of awareness to the importance

of good leadership and the existence of bad, so that I paid attention to the deliberate (or not) choices leaders make. He had the courage to have difficult conversations with compassion so that the message was understood and accepted. He advocated for his company in a way that was consistent with his values so it came across as authentic.

He was a voice of my conscience and provided good insight to whatever I was thinking about. He recently passed away, so I appreciate him even more for having taught me the gift of valuing and appreciating people in a very genuine way—not as boss/subordinate, but as human beings put on earth to support and help each other be their best.

Activates Potential

If we think back to those personal moments when the individual in charge indicated that "we were ready," one can surely recall the surge of enthusiasm and motivation to "get it done" and "get it right." Consider memorable "first times," for example, your first big presentation, the time you were first put in charge of a project, the first time you met with direct reports after becoming a supervisor, and so on. The Best Boss seems to dynamically support the activities of a direct report with relevant, just-in-time context, while simultaneously fostering a strong sense of empowerment for a direct report to do what he or she does best.

He gave me room to lead my own organization but was always available if I needed him.

Provides Pervasive Feedback

Feedback is a powerful catalyst in building preparedness for autonomous action. Feedback from the boss verifies to the employee that he or she understands and has mastered their tasks, and is ready to take on more. Consider the steps one must follow in earning a private pilot's license. In ground school, a student pilot learns about and then demonstrates basic understanding of meteorology, navigation, aircraft control and instrumentation, flight operations, and more. Then, the student pilot must master increasingly complex tasks in the presence of an instructor, literally earning the right to fly solo.

The individual can perform independently with confidence as the boss uses positive feedback to highlight notable work and constructive feedback to redirect performance when needed. Great sales managers periodically make joint calls with their sales staff, not to take over the call, but rather to provide reinforcement and coaching based upon direct observation.

> He was very vocal about my contributions and his high opinion of that work—both directly to me and to others in our firm.

Inspires Continuous Learning

Taking autonomous action involves risk of failure, for the boss and for the direct report. The Best Boss helps manage the employee's fear of making a mistake, or worse, their fear of failure, by reiterating that these situations provide the lessons for life-long learning, and both professional and personal growth, too. Furthermore, this balance of autonomy and learning occurs within the context of a boss who is there to support the individual and help him or her apply these lessons learned forward.

Being given the autonomy to chart one's own course provides more opportunity to take risks. thereby accelerating learning, even if the outcome falls short of the goal, or outright fails. The old adage that we learn more by failure than success is consistently true.

> He told me when I started the job that I was going to make mistakes, but as long as I kept him informed, he could work it out. He would give me his perspective, and for the most part, let me make the decision.

> He was always willing to support me. Regardless the situation, he had my back. I responded by making sure I never let him down and that included performing my job in such a way that my performance reflected positively on him.

Related Thinking

Modern thinking about worker motivation can first be traced back to the Hawthorne Studies conducted in the 1930s (Mayo 1945), followed by the publication of Maslow's hierarchy of needs (Maslow 1943).

The next theoretical landmark, emerging in the 1960s, was Douglas McGregor's Theory X and Theory Y (McGregor 1960). While these theories continue to dominate leadership literature, a number of theoretical and research-based points of view continue to emerge. For the purposes of our study, we selected just two more recent developments whose tenets clearly support the idea of promoting autonomy in leadership and worker motivation.

The first of these is flow theory. In his 1990 book, Csikszentmihalyi defines flow as

> A state in which people are so involved in an activity that nothing else seems to matter; the experience is so enjoyable that people will continue to do it even at great cost, for the sheer sake of doing it. This is an optimal state of intrinsic motivation, where the person is fully immersed in what they are doing. Flow is achieved when the level of task challenge is at or slightly greater than the skill level of the person, goals and required actions are explicit and feedback readily available (1990).

Flow theory explains why it is so engaging to play tennis or chess with an opponent who is at or slightly above our own skill level. It also explains the almost addictive nature of computer coding or programming work, or the popularity of computer-based games.

The conditions for flow clearly relate to the actions we have identified in characterizing the Best Boss. In promoting dynamic autonomy, a Best Boss will empower a direct report to take autonomous action in challenging arenas, work with the individual to set clear goals and expectations, and provide the comprehensive, pervasive feedback that will not only inform on progress, or the lack thereof, but will also build the employee's skills and competencies.

Subsequent to the emergence of the concept of flow, Daniel Pink offered a broader point of view on motivation and performance in his

2009 book entitled *Drive: The Surprising Truth about What Motivates Us*. Based on his review of past decades of research, he identified three key elements that must be considered: *autonomy, mastery,* and *purpose*. His point of view clearly coincides with our findings and conclusions. Consider Pink's observations:

- "This era doesn't call for better management. It calls for a renaissance of self-direction." (Pink 2009, p. 90)
- He cites research by Deci et al. who found "greater job satisfaction among employees whose bosses offered *autonomy support*." (2009, p. 89)
- "Autonomous people working toward mastery perform at very high levels. But those who do so in the service of some greater objective can achieve even more." (2009, p. 131)

Author Experience With Promotes Dynamic Autonomy

From John

John observed the art of Promotes Dynamic Autonomy at the top of several iconic American companies, including his organizational transformation consultant work with Jim Kilts. Following a long and successful career at Kraft (now Kraft-Heinz) where, for example, Mr. Kilts led the turnaround of Oscar Mayer through the successful introduction of "Lunchables," he led highly successful turnarounds of Nabisco and Gillette. Kilts' leadership approach is detailed in his 2007 book, *Doing What Matters,* as well as in a number of Harvard Business School cases detailing the Gillette turnaround.

In assisting Jim with his turnarounds, John developed a huge respect for his multifaceted approach to leadership. One of his most striking strategies was to never replace the cadre of C-suite officers he "inherited" when he became CEO. Instead, he explained his approach to the business (building Total Brand Value), worked with his direct report officers to help them understand this vision, and developed relevant objectives and the strategies to achieve them. He supported them as needed, but largely gave them full autonomy, then led quarterly performance reviews. This aspect was particularly intriguing, because it involved officers' self-evaluation, the peer evaluation of the other officers, and also Jim's evaluation. Jim once observed to John that:

> I never had to fire an officer—if they weren't successful in achieving their agreed-upon objectives over several quarters, they would voluntarily decide to leave the company.

Immediate Implications for the Workplace

As highlighted by the preceding quotes and examples, we see at least five immediate implications for leaders exhibiting the behaviors associated with this dimension of the Best Boss process:

- Given a clearer understanding of the "what" and the "why" of the business, we would expect direct reports to exhibit much better focus, alignment, and coordination of efforts.
- In addition, we would expect better-motivated direct reports to be much more likely to stay with the organization.
- Considering contemporary workplace challenges, Best Boss behaviors directly address the need for Millennials to have more autonomy in their work at an earlier experience level; the need for organizations to groom leaders at a younger age because of talent management challenges; and, the need to work more autonomously due to remote work.
- Given greater "dynamic" autonomy, we would expect enhanced innovation and creativity on the part of direct reports. Innovation is at the center of most organization's business goals as they try to compete in an increasingly complex world. Innovation will not be maximized without leaders fully embracing this dimension.
- Given the aforementioned, we would expect the organization to enjoy better individual and collective performance and results.

Self-Reflection

Take a moment and reflect on the extent to which "Promotes Dynamic Autonomy" is demonstrated in your behavior as a leader:

III.	Promotes Dynamic Autonomy: On a 5-point extent of use scale: To what extent do you typically exhibit this behavior?				
	Not at All	To a Small Extent	To Some Extent	To a Moderate Extent	To a Large Extent
	1	2	3	4	5

Instructions: Using the previous scale, write the number in the space to the left of each survey item that best represents your current use of the behavior. Next, calculate the average score and fill in the result in the space provided. At your option, you may use this information in Chapter 9 ("How to Become a Better Boss").

	Set clear expectations for direct reports in the "what" and "how" of getting their job done
	Provide direct reports the autonomy to do their job in the best way they can
	Help direct reports achieve a "big picture" view of the business and organization.
	Explain the work standards you expect direct reports to achieve
	Teach direct reports to work productively through organizational politics
	Take steps to improve direct reports' understanding of how the organization operates—both formally and informally
	Help direct reports understand the business the organization is in and their role within it
	Encourage direct reports to think and act strategically
	Share a vision of what you want to achieve
	Set clear goals and objectives for direct reports' work performance
(fill in average)	Average Extent of Use: Promotes Dynamic Autonomy

CHAPTER 7

Provides Pervasive Feedback

Definition

The Best Boss doesn't miss an opportunity to provide constructive and reinforcing feedback to the direct report.

Favorite Quotes From the Study

Regularly complimented my work and those around me, gave constructive criticism artfully—meaning, that I never felt corrected, just redirected!

Most importantly, perhaps, almost never missed a single feedback opportunity.

Helped me feel more confident when I was reaching beyond my 'comfort zone,' and was an honest mirror when I needed to see how others were perceiving me.

He was very direct in his feedback and would force me to look at my self-doubt in the eye and deal with it.

Discussion

This leader inherently understands that high performing individuals find feedback a "reward," in that it enables an individual to:

- Continue improving performance
- Derive personal satisfaction for work contributions and achievements
- Generate intrinsic motivation for improvement of future performance

In addition, candid and continuous feedback demonstrates transparency and trust, strengthening the relationship between the boss and the direct report.

Provision of feedback by the Best Boss was frequently mentioned by our respondents. It operates as a multifunctional performance and development enhancer in numerous ways, in that it affects perception of the boss, aids the employee enormously in the conduct of their work, and impacts the relationship in a variety of ways:

On the Boss

- Demonstrates the boss is paying attention
- Demonstrates the boss cares enough to take the time to share feedback

On the Employee

- Clarifies expectations and standards
- Acknowledges effective performance
- Provides direction for correcting or improving performance
- Provides task-specific as well as emotional support
- Contributes to motivation
- Builds self-confidence

On the Relationship

- Contributes to building the boss/direct report relationship
- Contributes to direct reports becoming better leaders themselves

For these reasons, the model would certainly be incomplete without the inclusion of feedback. In our view, pervasive feedback conveys significant information and guidance, as well as contributes to the immediate and longer-term motivation of the direct report.

The incorporation of feedback as part of the everyday relationship with an employee makes it much more meaningful and actionable, versus waiting for scheduled feedback sessions or an event-driven moment to discuss performance. Meaningful feedback includes positive recognition as well as coaching and constructive criticism.

Sharing valid feedback candidly and effectively also builds trust and strengthens the relationship between boss and direct report. Finally, the effect that providing feedback has *on the boss* should not be underestimated, either. It is no small feat to effectively discern, compose, and convey feedback. The process of providing feedback and observing its impact is a virtuous process for strengthening the skills, self-confidence, motivation, and effectiveness of the boss, too.

Igniting the System

Conveying feedback is clearly related to all other components of the Best Boss process:

Leads From a Higher Purpose

Taking the time to provide feedback, and even better, doing so again and again as simply part of the routine, clearly displays the values of the boss without him or her ever having to make this explicit: These actions "walk the talk."

> He delivered good news happily and always delivered the bad news as well. He did not shy away from difficult discussions that had to be had. He was not looking to be liked, he simply was who he was, which tended to have that result.

Activates Potential

Making the direct report aware of his or her potential is a key ingredient of activating potential. Feedback on performance and on expectations is one of the main ways of acknowledging and reinforcing present capability and future potential.

> He said, let's present this idea together. Help me think this through. What are we not thinking about?

Promotes Dynamic Autonomy

Feedback on performance and potential are thought to help set the parameters for independent action. Building awareness of strengths and building an employees' self-confidence helps establish a foundation for autonomous action.

> He paid attention to my work without smothering, correcting or overmanaging.

Inspires Continuous Learning

Feedback on both the positives and areas of improvement in current performance facilitates continuous learning. Building awareness of strengths, in turn, helps to build an employee's self-confidence, which is pivotal in encouraging risk-taking and hindering fear of mistakes.

> He helped me significantly during my formative years. I knew he was for me, yet in a very constructive way provided me with specific direct feedback that shaped who I am today and how I think about my work.

Related Thinking

On the Dearth of Feedback From Supervisors

When John briefly headed the Survey Research Program at the Human Resources Center of the University of Chicago in the late 1970s, he was dismayed to find a consistent survey statistic across organizations of all sizes and reputations. The survey question was "Does your boss provide you with sufficient feedback on your job performance?" and the response options were "agree," "undecided," or "disagree." The favorable responses were generally around 40 percent, indicating that 60 percent of employees either disagreed with or were undecided about receiving sufficient feedback on their performance. As a relevant benchmark, a 70 percent or higher favorable response on a question was seen as indicative of a high performing organization. Hence, many, if not most organizations would seem to "short change" employees on desired levels of feedback.

In their 2017 State of the American Workplace Report, the Gallup organization reported that:

- Only three in 10 U.S. workers strongly agree that in the last seven days they have received recognition or praise for doing good work. (p. 106)
- Only three in 10 U.S. workers strongly agree that in the last six months, someone at work has talked with me about my progress. (p. 120)

Results such as these evidence that not much has changed over the last 50 years, and that the provision of effective confirming and constructive feedback to direct reports remains a chronic "work in progress" for most bosses.

Benefits of Feedback

As an example, a 1980 study by Anderson and Level on downward communication in the *Journal of Business Communication* cited the following benefits of effective communication from the boss to the direct report:

- Better coordination
- Improved individual performance through the development of intelligent participation
- Improved morale
- Improved consumer relations
- Improved industrial relations (Anderson and Level 1980)

Focusing on performance feedback research published in four premier organization behavior journals over eleven years (1974–1984), Balcazar, et al. (1989) identified 126 applications of feedback in applied settings, and concluded that, among other things, "some characteristics of feedback are more consistently associated with improved performance than others," (p. 65) for example, the use of graphic/visual feedback, or supervisors/managers as the source of feedback delivery.

Alvero, et al. (2001) essentially replicated Balcazar et al.'s study for a 14-year period from 1985 to 1998, and identified 68 field application studies of performance feedback. Their findings corroborate those of Balcazar et al., but they observe that "The fact that we only found general agreement between reviews, especially in terms of feedback effectiveness, suggests that the characteristics of feedback may not be as critical as the way in which it is implemented" (p. 24).

We believe this observation, based upon their review of a quite substantial body of research, provides compelling testimony for the importance of Best Boss skills in providing effective feedback.

Employees Want Constructive Feedback

In their 2014 *Harvard Business Review* article on negative feedback, authors Zenger and Folkman cite the following findings from a survey of 899 U.S. and worldwide respondents:

- Roughly the same number of people prefer to give positive feedback as those who do not.
- Respondents preferred avoiding giving negative feedback while at the same time strongly preferred receiving negative feedback.
- In fact, the level of preference for receiving negative feedback was double that of receiving positive feedback.
- But how it was done really mattered—92 percent of the respondents agreed with the assertion, "Negative (redirecting) feedback, *if delivered appropriately,* is effective at improving performance" (Zenger and Folkman 2014).

Author Experience With Provides Pervasive Feedback

From John

John recalls a situation where the lack of pervasive feedback was a serious problem to a leading scientific and engineering professional services organization. A colleague who left consulting to become the Human Resources VP at a major consultancy in the United States requested assistance with an intractable problem facing his organization. Through exit interviews, he was learning that a major factor in employee dissatisfaction and turnover was the lack of feedback from the senior scientific staff to the junior consultants. Junior staff weren't developing as rapidly as required, in part because senior scientists felt no particular obligation to provide the constant, informal feedback which contributes to rapid development. The organizational norm seemed to be to avoid the topic until the annual performance evaluation, unless an employee merited being fired.

As a result, many junior staff were uncertain how their performance was viewed, afraid to speak up or ask questions, and felt they would have a more productive career development experience elsewhere. A multifaceted culture change process was initiated, including training in discerning, articulating, and delivering feedback "on the fly." Taking time for feedback became more of a regular practice, making measurable impact on development and retention.

Immediate Implications for the Workplace

The relationship between employee and supervisor is clearly the lifeblood connection between the employee and the organization. And, this relationship seems to strengthen, in part, through the inconspicuous, constant and supportive way that feedback is delivered by the Best Boss. We see three immediate implications, exemplified by quotes from our research:

Retention	"My supervisor's influence made me want to stay with the company, even as we grew bigger and less personalized. He had a way of always making me feel that my contributions were important to him. So, a job that I thought would last for a year or two ended up turning into a career of 24 years."
Engagement	"She always had an open door, gave informative positive and negative feedback, and had our backs. I worked harder and was willing to do more."
Performance	"I also felt like I wanted to validate his good opinion of me and the investment he made in my development. I never wanted to let him down. Impact on my performance was enormous. I consistently exceeded expectations and developed a reputation for being excellent with my clients and with my team."

Self-Reflection

Take a moment and reflect on the extent to which you demonstrate the dimension "Provides Pervasive Feedback" in your behavior as a leader:

IV.	**Provides Pervasive Feedback: On a 5-point extent of use scale: To what extent do you typically exhibit this behavior?**				
	Not at All	To a Small Extent	To Some Extent	To a Moderate Extent	To a Large Extent
	1	2	3	4	5

Instructions: Using the scale above, write the number in the space to the left of each survey item that best represents your current use of the behavior. Next, calculate the average score and fill in the result in the space provided. At your option, you may use this information in Chapter 9 ("How to Become a Better Boss").

	Promptly address, rather than avoid, difficult discussions concerning your direct reports' job performance
	Provide concrete evidence on the strengths of direct reports' performance
	Act in a fair-minded and straight-forward manner in your discussion of direct reports' work performance
	Serve as an honest mirror to convey how others perceive direct reports and their performance
	Appropriately compliment direct reports on their work
	Build trust by providing candid feedback on the strengths and areas for improvement of your direct reports' performance
	Serve as a skilled provider of feedback to direct reports
	Offer direct feedback and advice when your direct reports' performance is not up to par
	Take advantage of opportunities to provide useful feedback to direct reports
	Provide feedback continuously, in "real time," to direct reports, rather than waiting for formal performance evaluation discussions
(fill in average)	Average Extent of Use: Provides Pervasive Feedback

CHAPTER 8

Inspires Continuous Learning

Definition

The Best Boss acknowledges the inevitability of mistakes with a direct report, encourages discussion of them when they occur, and ensures lessons are mined for immediate learning.

Favorite Quotes From the Study

Once I made a really big error. It was costly. When I realized it, I went to my boss and said, "well you remember you told me we could work through mistakes and screwups?" He said, "yes" and then I told him what I had done. He said "sit down and let's see how we can solve this problem together." How did I feel? I think it is obvious. I returned his loyalty and trust and wanted to do the best job I could to help the company, my boss and the employees who worked with us. I wanted to be an example to others and help them grow and trust.

I felt empowered and engaged—and was excited to do my very best work. He gave me the appropriate amount of credit—and allowed me to shine—and make mistakes. He supported both with coaching.

Discussion

The Best Boss sets up a culture of continuous learning that fuels employee confidence in "embracing" the job in order to achieve results. The Best

Bosses in our study accomplished this by stating a very clear "philosophy of mistakes" to new hires:

> He told me when I started the job that I was going to make mistakes but as long as I kept him informed, he could work it out… On my first day on the job, my boss called me in his office to chat. We talked about a couple of things but what I remember most is he said, "There's not a mistake you can make that I can't handle so if something happens, let me know and we'll deal with it." That statement alone gave me the freedom to embrace my job without always looking over my shoulder and worrying about screwing up.

> When you make a mistake, just know I am here. It is okay. There isn't anything we can't work through. Just don't lie to me.

Further evidence showed that when mistakes occurred, Best Bosses would respond to them in very supportive and generative ways, (i.e., by using the mistake as an opportunity for the employee to learn and grow).

> He always had my back, but if I made a mistake, he would come to me and discuss 'other options.' I never felt like a failure. Mistakes were seen as part of the growth process in a person's life.

> When I made a mistake, he stood next to me, was not angry with me, but supported me and helped me understand how I could improve. He continues to be a mentor and close friend to me over the past 20 years.

> If I had a problem or made a mistake, [I felt comfortable] coming to him with it. He was going to help me through it and not just get down on me.

We are suggesting that a Best Boss uses mistakes as a platform to foster employee growth in combination with their own coaching behaviors in response to those mistakes made by their direct reports. We also hypothesize that this way of interacting diminishes tendencies of perfectionism in some that suppress learning, and hence, the achievement of results.

For example, excessive concern with perfection can result in an employee not taking on a task or speaking up when needed for fear of making a flawed contribution.

> Not only does he encourage me during my successes, he encourages me when I have made mistakes. I am a perfectionist and he helps me understand the importance of learning through mistakes. He is understanding and he relates.

Furthermore, we believe the Best Boss approach to mistakes increases the employee's propensity for taking calculated risks over time as a result of being freed from the fear of failure, as well as having increased opportunities to learn from experience.

> Empowered, I felt like I could take those "risks" and push myself. I wasn't afraid of making mistakes. I could work outside the box and try new things, new ways of working, etc. I used my creativity and no matter how silly something might seem to others, he would say "go for it."

Igniting the System

It's easy to see connections between "Inspires Continuous Learning" alongside the other dimensions of the Best Boss model. Additional study examples help illustrate the connection.

Leads From a Higher Purpose

A focus on fostering continuous learning is likely part of the value set held by many Best Bosses who have an implicit or explicit purpose to serve the interests of others. It takes leadership courage to place a direct report in a situation where a mistake could be costly to both the organization and a boss' reputation—just like the bosses we read about in Duncan's story (Chapter 5) who put him in his first solo meeting with the union when he was new to the labor relations role.

> You taught me to take chances, celebrate success, and appreciate that if I don't make mistakes, I'm not challenging myself enough.

He was the first person to totally trust me and say 'do what you want' and give me enough room to fail. And the first to support me if things didn't go the way I planned.

Activates Potential

A Best Boss who inspires continuous learning is likely to activate employee potential and perpetuate it, rather than deactivating potential by admonishing mistakes, thus creating fear and anxiety in their direct report. Consider a time in your life when the consequences of having made a mistake or reaching too far were demeaning or caused shame. While some people use this as a way to "stand up" to such critique from a boss, many if not most people simply feel defeated, demotivated, and/or less likely to take calculated risks.

Thanks for believing in me. Giving me the freedom to fail without the normal fear.

Promotes Dynamic Autonomy

The Best Boss finds opportunities to promote autonomy and learning simultaneously. This is accomplished by providing "just in time" coaching to an employee while providing critical contextual information the employee might need to succeed.

[In response to the question, what kinds of things would your Best Boss say or do?] "What went right? What went wrong? What would you have done differently? Do you understand the politics of this issue?"

Provides Pervasive Feedback

A natural appreciation for continuous learning highlights the desired nature of adaptive feedback—a point that can be lost on many leaders of people. For example, a Best Boss keeps the focus on learning by providing both confirmative and constructive feedback to the learner. Confirmative feedback tells the learner what he or she is doing correctly. Corrective feedback—incorrectly referred to as negative feedback—points out an opportunity to do better. Feedback provided in the context of continuous learning is experienced positively by employees, and eventually becomes a standard way of interacting at work.

> He would give praise where appropriate and give direct feedback when needed. He would share with me things I did well and offer advice when things didn't go as well. He wasn't condescending about it, just helpful...even when he was stressed to the max.

Related Thinking

It is likely that bosses who demean mistakes, or worse, make them anathema, may limit their employees' path to engagement at work. It is also conceivable that such a perspective limits an employee's freedom to innovate. Imagine 3M failing to capitalize on the "mistake" that led to Post-It notes? The story has it that in 1968, 3M employee Spencer Silver had mistakenly created a removable adhesive as opposed to the super strong one he had intended to create. While he came up with potential uses for it, 3M showed no interest in bringing it to market. Fast forward to 1974, when Arthur Fry, another 3M employee learned about the unusual adhesive at a departmental seminar being conducted by Silver. Fry thought of using the adhesive for keeping bookmarks from falling out of his choir hymnal. He helped convince senior leaders at 3M of the value of this new bookmark, and eventually they came around. The outcome is probably sitting in your desk drawer right now.

Beyond the Post-It note, the value of the mistake that led to the first implantable pacemaker is known to many. Back in 1956, Wilson Greatbatch, an adjunct professor of engineering, was attempting to build a device that would record heart sounds. He made a "mistake" by using the wrong transistor in the device, which gave off an electrical pulse, like that of the heart, instead of recording its sounds. Following his "mistake," Greatbatch sought out surgeon William Chardack, and by 1960, they were able to control the human heartbeat.

Our study and personal experiences suggest that Best Bosses who allow mistakes and coach through them are cultivating a robust belief system in their employees that ultimately leads to greater engagement and self-efficacy. In other words, the Best Boss shows the employee how to constructively think about and respond to what has gone wrong, instead of shutting down that resilient response by shaming him or her for making an error. This finding is consistent with the research being conducted by Carol Dweck on Growth Mindsets, previously discussed in Chapter 5 on activating potential: People with a growth mindset think of their talents and abilities as things they can develop through effort, practice, and instruction. Their trajectory is forward, not backward.

To understand the importance of this dimension and other learning-oriented dimensions of the Best Boss model, it is important to note that advances in neuroscience have shown the human brain to be plastic throughout life. Plasticity refers to the ability of the brain to change with learning and experience. This burgeoning field of study is in great contrast to the now-obsolete idea that as we age, the connections in the brain become fixed and then simply fade away. In essence, we are capable of learning throughout life. Organizations and other institutions not availing themselves of this human capacity are literally limiting themselves for positive change.

All of a sudden, we can begin to embrace the value of a boss, who, through shared philosophy and supportive behavior, cultivates a functional belief system and positive response to making mistakes on the job. And, the aspect of working through mistakes is pivotal. Stanford Graduate School professor and promoter of mathematics education reform, Dr. Jo Boaler, challenges outdated beliefs about how human beings learn and applies her research to the ways in which parents and others can promote learning in their children's lives.

Dr. Boaler suggests that people learn how to embrace struggle, mistakes, and failure *because* it fosters learning. As of January 26, 2021, *The Stanford News*, a publication of Stanford University Communications quoted Dr. Boaler:

> If you aren't struggling, you aren't really learning. When we're struggling and making mistakes, those are the very best times for our brains. Elizabeth and Robert Bjork, two scientists at UCLA who've been studying learning for decades, talk about the importance of "desirable difficulties," suggesting the brain needs to be pushed to do things that are difficult…When we embrace strug-

gle, it's freeing. It changes how we go about our work. We're more persistent. We interact with each other differently.

This perspective is consistent with our observation that a Best Boss inspires learning by sharing with a direct report that mistakes are understandable, and by coaching the employee through them, they are perhaps hard-wiring an approach to learning that can last a lifetime.

Author Experience With Inspires Continuous Learning

From Toni

I was lucky to have a boss who was really great in many dimensions of the Best Boss model, but in particular in "Inspires Continuous Learning." He was a fearless change agent and director of an internal consulting group with a strong vision. He empowered me and my team members in common pursuit by promoting continuous learning.

One way I continuously learned was by engaging with my boss in countless conversations of considerable depth regarding the company's history, strengths, business, and leadership challenges. He would describe this information in relationship to the strategy and direction of our internal group and with respect to my specific role and responsibilities.

Understanding that the currency of effective change management lies in the strength of relationships, this boss made it easy for me to learn about key individuals and networks throughout the organization. I will never forget the time he had an appointment with the Chairman of our Fortune 50 organization when he said, "you're coming with me." When we entered Chairman's office, the executive quickly removed his feet from the top of his desk upon seeing me with my boss. I was somewhat embarrassed, but at the same time, delighted and empowered—*the* leader whose support we would need most to effect change now knew my name.

Most importantly, my boss taught me how to take calculated risks, simply by unabashedly trying new approaches in change management without falling apart if they happened to turn out less than perfect. For example, we were signed up to support a reorganization in one of the operating companies as experts in transition management. We carefully identified key metrics for tracking the transition and displaying them for all to see. We had invented an enormous "metrics board" to bring to our initial client meeting, only to acknowledge its total obsolescence as we struggled to get it through the conference room door. Our facilitation of the meeting did not go much better, due to the fact that our industry knowledge was not up to par at the time.

Subsequently, the perfectionist in me was all too ready for a disparaging self-critique. Instead, my boss insisted on what he called a "structured debrief": What went right at the meeting, what went wrong, and how can we improve for next time? I found this incredibly helpful, and it promoted learning in real-time. Before long, we even found ourselves laughing at the absurdity of our metrics board.

For all the projects we worked on together, he shared credit in any outcome we achieved, whether it was failure or success. And every outcome, regardless of success or failure, was always followed by the debrief. Thus, we continuously learned from experience, which in turn fueled our confidence in trying innovative approaches to promote change in our company—which readily fed our appetite for further learning!

Immediate Implications for the Workplace

Much is lost to employee and organizational potential when leaders are not focused on inspiring continuous learning within their people. Without support when mistakes are made, an employee's focus is on avoiding mistakes rather than taking the types of risks that lead to creative and innovative outcomes. The reason for leaders *not* to provide support, in part, can be structural in nature. As an example, large spans of control and management jobs are often so densely designed with enough responsibilities for two positions, that even the most willing leader would find it hard to slow down to help an employee learn. Yet, slowing down to go fast is often precisely what is necessary for employee growth and organizational effectiveness. Other sources of "structural" interference could include lack of leadership development focused on helping managers cultivate a learning orientation in themselves and their people, or lack of reward systems that support managers who allocate time to promote continuous learning.

In any case, the consequences of failing to inspire continuous learning in employees is substantial. In fact, we believe the inspiration of continuous learning, activating potential, engagement, and retention go hand in hand, as discussed in earlier chapters. The leader who is unable to facilitate continuous learning—whether due to lack of time, interest, or competence—will impede the development of their reports, reducing engagement and decreasing the retention of a company's best talent, not to mention, the broader impact on the organization as a learning entity.

In summary, we may be likely to see more people leaders inspire continuous learning when:

- Learning is valued by the organization as an end in itself—a critical consideration, for what is an organization without employees who learn from experience and share continuously improving mental models with other employees? For more on this, see Daniel Kim's *The Link between Individual and Organizational Learning*.
- Jobs and spans of control are designed to allow time and opportunities to lead in such a way.
- Leaders of people, whether inclined or disinclined toward this dimension, are provided proper training and development; and
- Reward systems are aligned to reinforce all associated attitudes and behaviors.

When these areas are addressed from a leadership development perspective, benefits to organizational culture and business impact will undoubtedly follow.

Self-Reflection

Please take a moment and reflect on the extent to which "Inspires Continuous Learning" is part of your philosophical and behavioral repertoire.

V.	Inspires Continuous Learning (On a 5-point extent of use scale: To what extent do you typically...)				
	Not at All	To a Small Extent	To Some Extent	To a Moderate Extent	To a Large Extent
	1	2	3	4	5

Instructions: Using the scale above, write the number in the space to the left of each survey item that best represents your current use of the behavior. Next, calculate the average score and fill in the result in the space provided. At your option, you may use this information in Chapter 9 ("How to Become a Better Boss").

	Promote the notion that mistakes are opportunities for learning and not something to hide
	Teach direct reports to balance speed with effectiveness when it comes to making decisions
	Help direct reports extract the learning from mistakes they have made so the same mistakes won't be repeated
	Teach direct reports how to push the envelope in performing roles based on prior lessons learned
	Share examples of mistakes you have made to demonstrate to direct reports how a mistake can be used for learning and growth
	Show support when a mistake has been made
	Encourage direct reports to consider potential innovations that arise from mistakes
	Actively promote direct reports' learning through experience
	Establish a "philosophy of handling mistakes" with direct reports, to build trust and provide support for learning
	Conduct debriefings to fully identify and capitalize on the learnings from individual and team performance
(fill in average)	Average Extent of Use: Inspires Continuous Learning

CHAPTER 9

How to Become a Better Boss

In our experience, developing and implementing a personal action plan is the most direct route to upgrading your Best Boss skills and impact. We suggest a four-step self-development process, which is outlined in the following sections. These steps will be familiar to you, and you can decide how rigorously you will apply yourself in each of the following:

1. Assessment
2. Analysis
3. Action planning
4. Actualization

This process assumes you are analyzing with the intent to improve your overall leadership approach with direct reports. In some instances, however, you may want to complete this analysis and action-planning process separately for a specific employee who requires singular attention.

Step One: Assessment

The successful initiation of any improvement process requires a baseline and a focus. We offer two alternative methods that differ in time requirements and level of rigor to facilitate your initial assessment work.

Rigorous Self-Assessment

The first method is the more rigorous of the two. The concluding sections of chapters 4 through 8 each presented a set of self-reflection questions regarding your extent of use of the specific Best Boss behavior dimensions.

Table 9.1 Best boss behavior dimension extent of use scores and rank order of priority for improvement

	Extent of Use Score (Average of Ratings)	Rank Order of Priority
Leads from a Higher Purpose (Chapter 4)		
Activates Potential (Chapter 5)		
Promotes Dynamic Autonomy (Chapter 6)		
Provides Pervasive Feedback (Chapter 7)		
Inspires Continuous Learning (Chapter 8)		

You may or may not have replied earlier, so to complete a rigorous self-assessment, now is the time to turn back to those chapters and complete the self-reflections for each of the five dimensions.

Once your chapter self-reflection ratings are completed, simply add up and average the ten behavior ratings for each dimension, then fill in the totals in Table 9.1. Based on the dimension average, fill in the rank-order, with "5" assigned to the highest average score down to "1" for the lowest average score. These results indicate the emergent priority of attention on your journey to improved Best Boss proficiency—wherein the lowest average score is considered your highest priority for improvement.

In addition to filling in the average extent of use scores in Table 9.1, you may find it useful to construct a profile of your extent of use of these dimensions by entering the average scores in Figure 9.1. Place a dot on

RESULTS FOR:_____ DATE:_____

Leads from a Higher Purpose

Activates Potential

Promotes Dynamic Autonomy

Provides Pervasive Feedback

Inspires Continuous Learning

Overall Average Extent of Use

0   0.5   1   1.5   2   2.5   3   3.5   4   4.5   5

Figure 9.1 Best boss dimension extent of use profile

the point on the scale that corresponds to the average extent of use rating. A completed example is provided in the Appendix.

Quick Self-Assessment

You may be content with a more general, faster-paced initial assessment. One of our favorite methods is based on paired-comparison self-assessment. To try this approach, fill in your replies to this question in Table 9.2. Which of the two Best Boss dimensions in lines 1 through 10 in the following matrix do you most frequently exhibit in your on-the-job relationships with direct reports? Circle the one dimension title of the two in each line that you use most frequently. Then, for each column, total up the number of times you have selected that dimension. Finally, based on the dimension total, fill in the rank-order, with "5" assigned to the highest score down to "1" for the lowest score. (An example of the Quick Self-Assessment is presented in the Appendix.) These results indicate the emergent priority of attention on your journey to improved Best Boss proficiency, with the lowest score indicated as your highest priority for improvement.

To facilitate your decision making, we have provided a reminder of the definitions of each component of the Best Boss model below:

- *Leads from a Higher Purpose*: The Best Boss demonstrates a purpose beyond self and/or organizational interests by taking positive action on behalf of the direct report through an authentic relationship.
- *Activates Potential*: The Best Boss observes, values, acknowledges, and takes steps to activate the present capabilities and future potential of the individual.
- *Promotes Dynamic Autonomy*: The Best Boss imparts organizational knowledge and big picture thinking, establishes clear expectations, and creates an autonomous space for the individual to perform.
- *Provides Pervasive Feedback*: The Best Boss doesn't miss an opportunity to provide constructive and reinforcing feedback to the direct report.

Table 9.2 Paired-comparison evaluation matrix for frequency of use of best boss behavior dimensions

	Leads from a Higher Purpose	Activates Potential	Promotes Dynamic Autonomy	Provides Pervasive Feedback	Inspires Continuous Learning
1	Leads from a Higher Purpose	Activates Potential			
2		Activates Potential	Promotes Dynamic Autonomy		
3				Provides Pervasive Feedback	Inspires Continuous Learning
4	Leads from a Higher Purpose		Promotes Dynamic Autonomy		
5		Activates Potential		Provides Pervasive Feedback	
6			Promotes Dynamic Autonomy		Inspires Continuous Learning
7	Leads from a Higher Purpose			Provides Pervasive Feedback	
8		Activates Potential			Inspires Continuous Learning
9			Promotes Dynamic Autonomy	Provides Pervasive Feedback	
10	Leads from a Higher Purpose				Inspires Continuous Learning
Total Choices					
Rank Order 5= highest 1 = lowest					

- *Inspires Continuous Learning*: The Best Boss acknowledges the inevitability of mistakes with a direct report, encourages discussion of them when they occur, and ensures lessons are mined for immediate learning.

A close look at the assessment information established by one of the aforementioned methods provides both an initial baseline for your improvement planning as well as an initial focus for your consideration based on priority. All else being equal, the dimension that demonstrates your least utilized Best Boss behavior is the highest priority for your improvement plans.

Step Two: Analysis

We suggest two methods for a more in-depth analysis of your assessment results in order to set the stage for your improvement planning. Both methods assume that you've established an understanding of the *priority* of dimensions for your improvement attention. Given this understanding, the first method is based on a more careful examination of the individual behavior descriptions at the end of chapters 4 through 8.

Analysis Based on Self-Assessment

If you chose the more rigorous assessment approach, you have already considered your extent of use of specific behaviors in each dimension. If you chose the quick self-assessment, go back to the chapter that discusses your highest priority dimension to improve upon, and rate each behavior statement on the extent of use scale. Our belief is that any increase in extent of use of these less-frequently used behaviors will have a positive overall impact on your relationship with your direct reports.

Such changes in your behavior, however, will require much more than posting a note on your computer monitor as a reminder to demonstrate this behavior once each day. Some will require careful development of a relationship over time. For example, in the *Leads from a Higher Purpose* dimension, the behavior described as "work to get to know direct reports personally, not just as workers," will require time, the recognition of appropriate moments to discuss more personal matters, and even some note-taking to keep track of key aspects of a direct report's life outside of work, such as family, career aspirations, potential personal issues being faced, et cetera. In the "Provides Pervasive Feedback" dimension, successfully delivering the behavior described as "serves as a skilled provider of feedback to direct reports" in fact depends upon the development of observation, analysis, communication, and leadership skills that are certainly not developed overnight.

Working on the less-frequently-used behaviors of your highest priority dimension is a powerful way to begin your journey toward becoming a Best Boss. However, for those in search of more context and in-depth detail for behavior change, we offer a second analysis method based on informal interviews.

Analysis Based on Interviews

This method involves conducting an informal yet focused discussion with trusted confidants who are familiar with your working style and on-the-job behavior. In the discussion, you identify a behavior and ask for reactions, ideas, or suggestions as to how you might better approach this behavior in the future in order to be a more effective supervisor. For example, in the "Leads from a Higher Purpose" dimension, you may ask how, in your organizational situation, to better deliver the behavior described as "stand by your direct reports in practically every circumstance."

Your completion of one or both of these analysis suggestions will set the foundation in place for moving on to the action planning phase.

Step Three: Action Planning

The challenge in taking action to develop a stronger Best Boss skillset is to identify concrete behaviors that will make a difference in your relationships with employees, and that are sustainable over time. The analysis and interview work outlined in the prior sections are intended to provide useful ideas on necessary behavior changes. Additionally, before you begin to set specific objectives on a dimension-by-dimension basis, we offer some additional considerations on possible preparation and actions you can take to move forward. We conclude this section with a personal action-planning tool—the Best Boss Action Planning and Actualization Worksheets, to help focus and facilitate your own development. Finally, in the Appendix we provide several examples of analysis and completed worksheets so as to give you a useful point of reference.

Leads From a Higher Purpose

Managers seen as exhibiting strength in this area behave in ways to convey that while business results and/or successful personal performance matters, so do other value-based considerations. Coincidentally, this is often accomplished without ever talking about said values. Managers not seen as quite so strong in this area may define the job of "boss" more narrowly and may not have yet found a way to incorporate aspects of important personal or company values into their leadership style and behavior at work.

In this regard, author John is reminded of an executive he worked with as a consultant:

At the time I first met him, he was a mid-level financial manager. His usual behavior seemed to match the finance stereotype—the only thing that seemed to matter was the numbers. Imagine my surprise when later in his career, after he became a CEO, he emerged as a national advocate of children with special needs—an activity he had been involved in all along. He was highly respected by his people, and my guess is that—spoken or not—these values impacted his on-the-job behavior. Not surprisingly this organization became known as a best place to work.

Developmental suggestions related to *Leads from a Higher Purpose:*

- Conduct a "personal values exercise" where you examine the alignment between your own values vs. the values of your company.
- Define your personal leadership philosophy.
  - Share your philosophy, beliefs, and values with your direct reports and discuss how to put them into action within the company culture.

- Take time to reflect on the way you spend (or fail to spend) time with direct reports.
- Conduct an "ethics in our current business environment" meeting with direct reports, based upon the company's code of ethics.
- Talk with respected colleagues about how they act out their values both at work and in their lives, and what these values are.
- Identify "missed opportunities" in your own career where your behavior did not align with your own "higher purpose."
- Reflect on the extent to which your own Best Boss demonstrated higher purpose and/or values in their working relationship with you.
- Imagine you were composing a story about higher purpose from your work experience to tell a child or grandchild. What led up to the situation, what did you and others do, and what was the result?
- In one of his books, author Peter Drucker suggests that annually, managers should conduct a time log exercise to examine how they are spending their time. Whether or not you choose to undertake such an exercise, what would your daily or weekly use of time tell us about your values?

Activates Potential

Managers that are particularly effective in this area behave in a way that conveys a strong belief in the potential of their employees, show determination to bring out "the best" in their performance, and have a knack for arranging suitable developmental opportunities. Managers that are less effective in this area may not believe they have sufficient time (e.g., due to large span of control) or skill to get to know, much less figure out how to further develop an employee. In addition, they may not want to risk nominating an employee for a developmental opportunity, lest poor performance reflect back upon them as the employee's sponsor. Lastly, some managers are simply unwilling or do not understand the value in taking on the responsibility for a direct report's development beyond what is absolutely necessary to do the job at hand.

Developmental suggestions related to *Activates Potential:*

- Get to know more about the capabilities and developmental needs of your direct reports via one-on-one meetings (beyond traditional performance reviews), luncheon discussions, or simply stopping by their work station for a chat.
- Request that direct reports prepare a written description of their desired next career step (e.g., one to three years out), and the strategies they believe will get them there. Then, work with them over time to assist them in moving toward these goals.
- Actively seek opportunities to showcase the talents of direct reports:
  - Stretch assignments
  - Participation in corporate initiatives
  - Invitations to meetings at the next level
  - Training or mentoring others in areas of special expertise
- Solicit input and suggestions from direct reports on various issues and directions you are considering, or problems and opportunities you are addressing.
- Conduct a talent assessment of each of your direct reports to establish estimates of sustained performance and potential (e.g., learning agility, resiliency, leadership potential, aspirations, etc.).
- Candidly convey your views of a direct report's potential to him or her, and seek their input on situations or assignments that could help them better realize their own potential.
- Engage colleagues in a candid discussion of their perception of direct reports' potential and solicit their suggestions for better realization of this potential.
- Share stories with your direct reports about how your own Best Boss provided you with experiences and opportunities to better realize your potential.

Promotes Dynamic Autonomy

Highly effective managers regularly convey knowledge, business acumen, and "big picture" thinking, establish clear expectations, and allow direct reports the freedom to perform their roles. Establishing an understanding of context, providing perspective on industry and organizational dynamics, and conveying confidence in their ability to "get it and act accordingly" are the hallmarks of this dimension. This leader does all he or she can to create a context in which a direct report can optimally execute their responsibilities. In contrast, less effective managers have difficulty communicating the "big picture" and may even engage in micromanaging. In part, this may result from the boss' own lack of understanding of the "big picture," much less the challenge of conveying this understanding in terms that are meaningful to an employee in the context of their specific role within the organization. Finally, a high need for control and difficulty in tolerating uncertainty will dampen a manager's enthusiasm for granting autonomy.

Developmental suggestions related to *Promotes Dynamic Autonomy*:

- Work to ensure that a "line of sight" between organizational goals and the direct report's work objectives is fully understood. This includes being mindful of the organization's formal objectives-setting processes, as well as your own informal management practices. Important elements to consider include:
    - Definition of annual objectives and performance standards for direct reports and discussion of their relationship to company direction
    - Provision of feedback and coaching
    - Making your expectations for communications and performance explicit (e.g., how often do you want to hear from employees and on which topics)
- Conduct periodic strategy update sessions with your direct reports during which you reinforce the company's vision and values, strategic direction, and update on progress toward diverse goals (operational, financial, people, etc.)

- Twice per year, hold a meeting with direct reports to review and discuss the external landscape, including information on economic, regulatory, competitor, workforce, consumer, and customer trends.
- Reorganize your work processes to increase opportunities for greater individual self-initiated action and autonomy for direct reports, for example, allocating one full day per month to pursue a self-defined initiative or project.
- Sponsor contests and/or "friendly" competitive events to foster identification of individual, team, and work group autonomous action opportunities.
- Regularly allocate one-on-one discussion and team discussion time to share stories of successes, failures, and lessons learned in relation to taking autonomous action.
- Conduct a RACI analysis of your job and your direct report's job to provide a foundation for autonomous action (isssp. org/the-raci-chart-simply-explained). This acronym RACI (Responsible, Accountable, Communicate, Informed) identi-fies a process for clarifying job responsibilities in any job.
- Seek input from your direct reports on which parts of your job they feel ready to take on; then, create opportunities for them to do so.

Provides Pervasive Feedback

Managers that are particularly effective in this area consistently and unabashedly utilize multiple approaches to feedback in their interactions with direct reports. These approaches fall along many continua, including:

- From direct (e.g., "here's what you did that worked, and here's what you did that needs to improve…") to indirect (e.g., "let's let the consequences of your actions tell us both whether or not they were effective…")
- From formal (e.g., included in the annual performance review) to informal (e.g., "as I was passing by your desk, I was reminded to tell you how thorough and well-organized

your analysis presentation came across in the senior management meeting…")
- From quantitative (e.g., "your revenues are up by 20 Percent")
to subjective (e.g., "when you conveyed your point of view, it
made me feel proud to be your boss…)"

It is particularly important that the feedback be valid, candid, timely,
and presented respectfully using communication approaches that are
appropriate to the employee and the setting.

Author John Furcon recalls one of his favorite personal feedback experiences with his consulting career Best Boss:

> She asked if she could conduct my annual performance review
> meeting while completing a four-mile jog at a client's residen-
> tial conference center in Wisconsin. I thought it would be quite
> "interesting," so, of course, I agreed. Happily, while the setting
> was quite unconventional, the content of the discussion was
> mostly positive, and by the time she was finished, I felt fully rec-
> ognized, highly appreciated and was "basking in the glow" of the
> experience. However, part of the reason this event stands out so
> vividly in my memory is the fact that, at this point in our run,
> two German Shepherd watchdogs came running down an adja-
> cent driveway in hot pursuit—of us. Fortunately, the owner was
> nearby and called them back, and they turned out to be large pup-
> pies, not the ferocious animals we initially perceived. So much the
> better if feedback can be tied to a "significant emotional event!"

Developmental suggestions related to *Provides Pervasive Feedback*:

- Make provision of multidimensional feedback a part of your
daily routine with each of your direct reports.
- Begin asking colleagues for feedback on your own
performance and take note of how this impacts your
own motivation, learning, and growth:
  ○ Ask what was favored about what you did in a specific
  situation, and why?

  - º What opportunities for improvement does the respondent note?
  - º What additional advice for improvement would he or she offer?
- Seek feedback on your performance from direct reports in order to build their awareness around the key details of performance as well as the handling of the feedback process.
- Use "after action" discussions with your colleagues and direct reports to highlight the positives and areas of improvement for individual and work group performance.
- Organize formal and informal recognition events to describe, highlight, and celebrate individual and team successes.

Inspires Continuous Learning

Managers who are highly effective in this dimension love to encourage learning—even in the context of mistakes and calculated risk—for the dual purposes of achieving great business results and continuous personal and professional growth. They understand the tremendous learning opportunities that await when situations fall short of expectations or in situations where genuine mistakes and oversights have occurred. A virtuous cycle of performance is cultivated by establishing a "philosophy of mistakes" between the leader and employee that includes early identification and sharing of mistakes or problems, followed by analysis, correction, and the application of learning going forward. The propensity for taking the risk grew out of the learning, and the learning occurred because the boss allows for mistakes.

When questioned by a reporter about his many failed experiments, Thomas Edison is reported to have replied, "I have not failed, not once. I've discovered ten thousand ways that don't work."

Less effective managers demonstrate maladaptive behaviors in response to mistakes, appearing less concerned with learning and more concerned with blame or punishment. The inevitable result is a culture wherein making a mistake is housed in fear that, in turn, limits learning and even the taking of reasonable risks based upon real-time learning.

Developmental suggestions related to *Inspires Continuous Learning*:

- Use "after action" discussions with your colleagues and direct reports to highlight the positives and areas of improvement for individual and work group mistakes and problems in performance.
- Use both financial and nonfinancial rewards to acknowledge behavior and performance that is consistent with continuous learning along with your "philosophy of mistakes;" for example:
  - When someone brings a mistake to your attention, positively acknowledge the behavior as a part of your process of working through the mistake.
  - Take time to recognize and celebrate advancements and improvements that are traced back to learning from an earlier mistake, , for example, Fleming's discovery of penicillin when a laboratory dish was accidentally left uncovered.
- Understand and be able to articulate the significance of continuous learning and the relationship between reasoned risk-taking and learning.
- Share stories of effective risk-taking from your functional area, business, science, current affairs, or history that illustrate the learning and performance outcomes from thoughtful and considered risk-taking. For example, the first heart catheterization was performed when a physician inserted a catheter into his own vein and guided it into the right chamber of his heart, and then X-rayed himself to prove it had been accomplished.
- Share stories of continuous learning and risk-taking successes and failures from your own career, including the lessons you derived from those experiences.

We trust this more detailed review of the key behaviors involved in each of the five Best Boss dimensions has helped further illustrate the intent behind those dimensions. The ideas for specific actions you can take to further develop and demonstrate desired Best Boss behaviors will set a strong foundation for your own action planning.

Best Boss Action Planning and Actualization Worksheets

Action Objectives and Plan

These worksheets provide a simple framework to focus and sustain your journey toward mastering Best Boss behaviors. Additional original copies are included in the Appendix along with a completed example to facilitate your weekly planning and activities over as many weeks as it takes to reach your desired level of mastery.

Step 1: Based on your self-assessment and review in this chapter, please identify between two and three of the most important areas for development and write the dimension titles in the chart below.

Step 2: Next, for each dimension chosen, identify up to three of the lowest-rated behaviors in the respective dimensions

---

	Priority	Top Priorities for Development
	Dimension title	Lowest rated dimension behaviors (up to 3 per dimension)
1		
	Dimension title	Lowest rated dimension behaviors (up to 3 per dimension)
2		
	Dimension title	Lowest rated dimension behaviors (up to 3 per dimension)
3		

Step 3: For each prioritized behavior, create a weekly action plan using the forms provided

Plan for Week _____

Behavioral objective	What I plan to do this week		
From the Priority List mentioned earlier, choose a low-rated behavior to address this week and write it in the space below:	Get specific on what you plan to do as it pertains to this behavior:		
Dimension title: Behavior:	Who: What: Where: When: Why:		
Learning partner	**Supportive stakeholders**	**Contingent reward for success**	**End of week Self-rating 10=high; 1=low**
Who will be your learning partner for this objective that will observe you in action and provide feedback?	Who will you identify as key stakeholders for moral support?	How will you reward yourself if you make notable progress this week?	Based on input from others and your own self-observation, how would you rate progress on this objective?

Step Four: Actualization

In this concluding section, we present a few ideas, suggestions, and mechanisms for ensuring your desired Best Boss behaviors are self-sustaining over time. Simply stated, three factors are at play when you attempt to change your behavior:

- *Knowledge*: This includes information and insight. Hopefully, your review of our research results provides useful insights; your assessment and action-planning work provides information. The challenge, of course, is converting knowledge into action.

- *Skill*: We can achieve an intellectual grasp of many activities, but successful performance of complex activities requires practice and skill development. In his 2008 book *Outliers,* Malcolm Gladwell popularized the findings of psychologist Anders Ericsson, which set the 10,000 hours of practice standard for becoming truly expert at some activity. Later research suggests that focused, intense practice requires less time to achieve comparable levels of mastery. Our point here is that you will likely require quite a bit of practice to get *really* good at your desired Best Boss skills.
- *Attitude and motivation*: Colin Powell famously observed that "attitude is a force multiplier." We can get a lot more done if we understand and leverage our own motivational dynamics. It may be something as simple as "I do my best thinking and writing in the morning," to something as complex as "the continued existence and success of my work group depends upon my ability to get everyone on board with these needed changes." Considering both the extrinsic (e.g., financial, reputational) and the intrinsic (e.g., sense of accomplishment, mastery or contribution) rewards will be key in your realization of desired changes in your own behavior. What will it take to get you moving and keep you moving in pursuit of your desired behavior changes?

Our favorite tools for supporting behavior change include the following:

- *Put it in writing*: Writing out your objectives and plans has been found to increase the likelihood of following through on them.
- *Chart your progress*: Calendars, wall charts, Gantt charts, dashboards, and the like provide visual reinforcement and sustain motivation.
- *Go public*: Sharing your objectives with key stakeholders in your work and in your life will help keep you motivated.

- *Enlist a buddy (or two!)*: The value of personal support in making behavior changes is well documented in many aspects of life, including the overcoming of addiction in the 12-step rehabilitation program.
- *Engage the services of a professional coach*: Used for decades by leading organizations to facilitate the development of C-suite successors, research shows that one-on-one coaching work with an experienced executive coach over a period of six months to a year has a significant impact on the behavior and business impact of the coaching client.
- *Celebrate successes*: Give yourself credit for progress as the journey unfolds.
- *Consider the wisdom of the ages* including "Life is a journey, not a destination" (Ralph Waldo Emerson).

CHAPTER 10

Jeff's Story: Perspective From a Baby Boomer[1]

"Jeff" received his bachelor's degree in Behavioral Science followed by his next academic achievement, a master's degree in Industrial/Organizational Psychology. Upon graduation with his advanced degree, he landed a Human Resources position with a corporate regional office. 25 years later, he was appointed Chief Executive Officer of the entire corporation and its 20,000 employees. Huh?! How did that happen? The answer, in part, is to have a Best Boss like his boss, "Edgar." When Jeff started his first job, he assumed his career would be in Human Resources. And that would have made him perfectly happy. But everything changed when Edgar became his boss. Jeff and Edgar had a similar Midwestern background which made for an easy, instant connection. Early on in their relationship, Edgar noticed Jeff's potential well before Jeff noticed it himself. He gave Jeff projects that were beyond the typical boundaries of an HR role and ultimately offered him an operations role assignment outside of the Human Resources department. Moving from HR to such a technical role was a daunting proposition for Jeff; so, before he made his decision, he wanted to talk with some people to get their objective opinion on making such an unconventional move. Among those he spoke with was a consultant who had worked with the organization for many years, and thus understood the culture quite well. The consultant forewarned Jeff that taking this new job would be a big mistake. In fact, he used the term "career derailer" as he told Jeff it would be another example of the organization "chewing up" good talent.

Needless to say, Jeff was a little rattled by these conversations. Edgar, on the other hand, remained undaunted, reassuring him that he had

---

[1] Names and organizations in this story were changed to provide anonymity.

no doubt Jeff would be successful in the role. As with Courtney from our story in Chapter 1, Jeff felt Edgar's confidence in him was undeserved. However, his unfettered trust and faith bolstered Jeff in a way that inspired him to have confidence in himself. Jeff ultimately accepted the new role, and it was one of the best experiences of his life. He had a new career trajectory all because Edgar had the foresight to see Jeff's potential and the commitment to help him realize that potential himself.

Jeff worked ten more years for Edgar until his retirement, at which time Jeff was promoted to CEO. And, although the "official" working relationship between Edgar and Jeff had ended, the mentoring continued when the company was acquired by larger corporate entity. Shortly after the acquisition, Jeff was confronted with an unsettling surprise when one of his key leaders, mentees and someone Jeff really cared about on a personal level, resigned suddenly. Jeff remembers being moved to tears when he was informed of this individual's decision to leave. He made a quick telephone call to inform his wife of the bad news. Following that conversation, Jeff received a call from Edgar. Immediately, a dispirited Jeff shared the news of his mentee's departure, and after listening quietly, Edgar told him to *"fill the box."* Jeff didn't understand what he meant, so Edgar said it again. *Fill the box.* Jeff became irritated, telling Edgar he didn't have time for puzzles.

As it turned out, this small riddle became one of the most important leadership lessons of Jeff's life. Essentially, Edgar told Jeff that he must focus on the problems he can control. As Edgar put it, "Your mentee has made a decision and is moving on. That's what you need to do as well. You must focus on the forward problems that you and the organization are facing, not the backward ones that you cannot do anything about."

But that wasn't the end of the story. As it turns out, this situation provided Edgar an opportunity to share more wisdom with Jeff. But this time, it was not a lesson for Jeff, the leader, but a lesson for Jeff the person. About a week after the "fill the box" episode, Edgar called Jeff to check in. He told Edgar that he was focused and looking forward again, and that it was all because of him. Edgar's only was response was admonishment as he asked Jeff whether he had learned anything at all from his years of Edgar's mentorship and friendship. Jeff was befuddled.

Then, Edgar said, "are you not aware that as soon as your wife hung up with you, she called me? She knew you were suffering and needed some advice. So, if you have anyone to thank, it's not me; it's your wife."

Edgar was a special guy. Was he perfect? Nope. Did he get it right all of the time? Not a chance. Did Jeff argue with him? Absolutely. But Edgar was Jeff's Best Boss, someone special, and someone who saw his potential, someone that had an immeasurable impact on Jeff's career and life. Jeff will never forget him. Neither will his wife.

CHAPTER 11

Why Best Bosses Matter

Over the course of the past few years, we have done several Best Boss workshops and webinars where, among other things, we share our study insights. Once we have fully explained and discussed the Best Boss Leadership dimensions, we ask the audience if anything about the dimensions came as a surprise to them. Typically, there is no response. Not because they are bored (at least we hope not!) or need a bio break, but because there really is nothing groundbreaking about them. Throughout our research, we found that Best Bosses trust and respect their people. They have strong, positive values, focus on development, feedback, autonomy, and learning. They are supportive when mistakes are made and give praise on a regular basis. This all makes sense, right? So, does this kind of leadership really matter?

As Table 11.1 displays, nearly all of our study respondents suggested their performance excelled under their Best Bosses. More than three quarters felt a strong engagement with the work they performed and a positive impact on their skill development and/or careers. More than one-third of survey respondents told us that their Best Boss taught them how to

Table 11.1 Direct report impacts identified in the best boss study

Impact On ...	Data
Individual Performance	93 percent of respondents said their performance excelled while working for their Best Boss
Level of Engagement	82 percent of respondents made statements or used terms that indicated high engagement
Career / Skill Development	77 percent of respondents said their Best Boss had a positive impact on their development
Ability to Lead	36 percent of respondents made a direct statement on how their Best Boss made them a better leader
Personhood	24 percent of respondents made a direct statement on how their Best Boss helped them become a better person

lead—potentially leaving a people leadership legacy in their wake. And, nearly 25 percent of our survey respondents showed that the influence of Best Bosses can transcend organizational boundaries. These respondents felt a direct impact on who they became as people, beyond the workplace, as a result of their experience with their Best Bosses.

Combining our data analysis with relevant external information and our collective professional experience, we identified four ways leaders with a Best Boss leadership profile can positively impact the organization and the individual. First, they help create a *connection* or bond between the organization and employee that enhances engagement and retention. Second, they lay the groundwork for exceptional *performance and achievement.* Third, they can develop a *legacy* of great leadership by teaching others how to lead, potentially "paying it forward" when Best Boss direct reports begin to lead others. Fourth, they leave a *lasting impact on our life and our lives* by positively influencing our values while also enriching our health and well-being.

Let's explore these four impacts.

Creating a Connection

Take a moment to consider the following from Gallup (2017):

- One in two U.S. adults have left their job to get away from their manager and improve their overall life at some point in their career.
- Managers account for at least 70 Percent of the variance in employee engagement scores across business units. This means the great majority of impact on engagement has the boss as its main source.

If it's true that people tend to quit their jobs or are less engaged because of a bad boss, then you could argue that the inverse is worth considering. That is, people would be inclined to stay with their company because of a great boss. This was certainly true with Joel, whose story we shared in our introduction. Not only did he stay at a company with which he did not feel a strong connection, but we later discovered he subsequently followed and worked for this same person two more times throughout his career. Some of our survey participants made the same observation:

> [My Best Boss] inspired me to continue working for this company, even though the owners and other executives could be inconsiderate and demeaning.

> [My Best Boss]'s influence made me want to stay with the company, even as we grew bigger and less personalized. He had a way of always making me feel that my contributions were important to him. So, a job that I thought would last for a year or two ended up turning into a career of 24 years.

As we discussed in Chapter 5, Activates Potential, the employment "contract" for previous generations—which provided employment security, reliable compensation, and career opportunities in exchange for employee loyalty—has largely evaporated. While these concepts are still part of an individual employment retention decision, they don't have the same gravitational pull as they did before. The net result is that many of us have become predisposed to leave our companies rather than to stay, leaving organizations more at risk than ever of losing the very talent they need in order to stay competitive.

It is our firm belief that leaders with a Best Boss profile are a hedge against this risk of unwanted employee turnover for two reasons. First, because of their focus on activating potential, Best Bosses help individuals learn, develop, and grow, which helps them maintain a contemporary set of skills and competencies that keeps them in demand amid an ever-competitive talent marketplace. This is supported by the data in Table 11.1 which shows that over 75 percent of survey respondents felt that their Best Boss had a positive impact on their development and thus their career. Second, and perhaps more important, our study shows that Best Bosses build a trusted and personal relationship with their employees, which naturally creates a positive connection with the employing organization.

Given these contemporary norms governing work and careers, employees won't stay with an employer for the duration of their career as they typically did a generation ago. It is, however, a strong possibility that they will stay longer if they work for a person who brings the Best Boss leadership dimensions and behaviors into their leadership of others. In turn, as we noted earlier, employees will be more likely to be engaged.

Laying a Foundation for Achievement

Of all our survey questions, of particular interest is the inquiry regarding the impact of a Best Boss on individual performance. For many leaders, and organizations, this is an important aspect of our survey that should move the Best Boss findings from interesting to actionable. Why? Because of the common belief that engaged employees perform better. And in our survey analysis we saw compelling evidence that Best Bosses forged more engaged employees which, in turn, may drive superior performance. In fact, 93 percent of our respondents acknowledged that their work performance excelled while working for their Best Boss. They felt *obligated* to exceed expectations because the bond with their Best Boss was so important to them. Letting their Best Boss down was unthinkable.

I have never worked harder or had more challenging successes than when I worked for (my Best Boss). I gave him and the organization 150 percent if not more.

I felt that I had to raise the bar even higher.

I wanted to go to the mat for [my Best Boss]. I wanted to do my very best so that I would not let him down.

While we rely on our respondents self-reporting as evidence of superior performance, we ask you to consider your own performance when you worked for your Best Boss. Could one of these quotes echo your own thoughts about personal performance while working for this special person?

External data support the notion that engaged employees produce results. Gallup (2017) found that highly engaged business units realize a 41 percent reduction in absenteeism and a 17 percent increase in productivity. Salesforce surveyed over 1,500 business professionals on values-driven leadership and workplace equality. They discovered that when an employee feels heard, that person is 4.6 times more likely to feel empowered to perform to the best of their abilities. The National Bureau for Economic Research (2012) found that the work teams of good bosses outperformed those teams led by bad bosses by 10 percent.

It was particularly interesting to read how individuals described their performance while working for their Best Boss. People were inspired to go *above and beyond* expectations. They brimmed with confidence, which allowed for greater effort and risk-taking—and they consistently wanted to do more. Perhaps most importantly, they focused on how their Best Boss helped them aspire to and realize their fullest potential, which in turn, allowed them to play an integral role in both team and company performance.

> Because of my best boss's support, I feel more confident in my skills and in the work I accomplish. I also feel better prepared to handle challenging assignments and perform work that may be outside of my comfort zone.

> My best boss's encouragement and trust in me caused me to go above and beyond the expectations of the job. For that reason, I grew in ways that I never expected. My work was often difficult but always left me feeling accomplished and good about what I was doing.

> I worked so hard for (my Best Boss) and the organization.

Leaving A Legacy

A couple years ago, Rick, a Vice President for a global retail organization was reflecting on his Best Boss experience. He described his manager, George, with familiar Best Boss leadership themes. As a result, Rick observed, "You know, not a week goes by that I don't ask myself, what would George do?" Imagine that! Here was Rick, a seasoned senior executive who had not worked for his Best Boss in over fifteen years, and he was still using him as his measuring stick for great leadership. Rick felt an obligation to be the best possible leader because of George's exceptional tutelage. He never wanted to fall short of George's expectations. Often, people will carry the lessons from their Best Boss deep into their own careers as leaders.

> I became a far better leader thanks to [my Best Boss]. I look at problems differently—they are challenges. I look at opposing positions differently, I can learn from them. I need to understand other perspectives in order to be sure that my position is reasonable. I try to reach out to individuals in polarized situations. I always make decisions that I can be proud of from a business perspective as well as personal. If those conflict, I have learned to keep digging, there are usually better answers.

> Through my experience of working for [my Best Boss], I now have no excuses for not treating my subordinates as he treated me, given the very positive response I had to his tutelage.

In Chapter 4, we shared the story of Peggy Troy, and how she carried on the leadership legacy established by her Best Boss, Gary Schorr. This legacy has been passed along to Peggy's direct reports. We had the opportunity to interview Rob Sanders, Chief Administrative Officer, Bob Duncan, Executive Vice President, and Laura Miller, Vice President Planning (Rob and Laura have since left their positions) and it was clear their leadership philosophy and approach was directly connected to the relationship with Peggy, just as Peggy's was connected to Gary's. In fact, this philosophy has become ingrained in the culture of the hospital overall, which emphasizes the critical influence the top executive's leadership style and approach has on organizational culture.

Another finding we noticed in our study is that, in addition to learning about great leadership from their Best Boss, some people had a powerful sense of obligation to *carry forward* those leadership lessons as a personal testament to the individual who had been such an inspirational mentor to them. As was noted in our earlier story from Rick, in discussing leadership legacy, people do not want to disappoint their Best Boss when they are working for them, and they don't want to fall short of their teachings later on when they are leaders themselves. As one survey respondent eloquently told us,

I would tell my favorite boss that he had a profound effect on me and helped to shape me as a professional, as a leader, as a contributor, and as a teammate. The experience of working with him, literally, changed the course of my career and helped me understand how to pull the best out of myself and others. I would thank him for that and for being a constant and consistent mentor, coach, and friend. We all need those few individuals who play that role for us, both in the direct boss/subordinate relationship and beyond, across the lifespan of our careers. I would also tell him that I have worked hard to pay it forward, to be that individual for others coming up in their careers. I hope I have done you justice.

Such quotes reinforce the potentially long-lasting and positive repercussions a Best Boss can have on other leaders. This topic was also explored by authors Brooks, Stark, and Caverhill in 2004. They spent five years speaking to a cross section of men and women from all walks of life, asking them who had left an indelible impression in their lives, and more importantly, why. Often, they found, it was organizational leaders who had positively made a difference. Here is an excerpt from their book's introduction:

If you influence change in the lives of those around you, you are engaged in an act of leadership. Your leadership legacy is the sum difference you make in people's lives. directly and indirectly, formally, and informally. Why should you care about your leadership legacy? As a leader, you will impact your people and they will take what they learn forward into the future of your organization. The challenge is how to live in a way that creates a legacy that will make a positive difference in the lives of those around you.

Impacting a Life

Many people touch our lives. A select few of those people have a profound influence on who we are and who we become as individuals. Some of us are lucky enough to have a Best Boss who helps us become not just a better employee, but a better person. Do you recall how Courtney described the impact Bob had on her life in Chapter 1? It's worth repeating this quote from her:

> Words cannot express what your support, mentorship, guidance, and friendship have meant to me all of these years. I would not be the professional or person I am today without you and all you have given me. I am incredibly grateful, appreciative and privileged to have known and worked with you. I will take everything you have taught me into all of my future roles in work and life as a colleague, friend, wife, and mother.

In some cases, Best Bosses can impact lives far beyond the workplace, which is exemplified by the following story taken from Duncan's work experience.

Amanda and Joe

It's not always easy to summon the courage to take a stance that you know could run the risk of damaging your standing in an organization. But, if you are a leader, courage must be part of the job description. And, when exercised, courage in leadership can have ripple effects that expand farther than you could have imagined, even reactivating the potential of a mid-career employee who seemed to be a lost cause.

It was the first sales meeting for Amanda as the newly-appointed Midwest Regional Sales Vice President. She knew all eyes would be on her to see if this up-and-coming young woman would have what it takes to lead a large group of male, veteran, and somewhat crusty sales managers. The group gathered the night before for a premeeting dinner. Alcohol flowed freely. About midway through the dinner, Amanda noticed that one of the sales managers, Joe, was visibly intoxicated. As the evening wore on, he became loud and belligerent, yet no one seemed bothered. As Amanda later found out, this drunken behavior had become accepted by the group. While the evening ended without incident, Amanda was concerned.

The following morning, before the sales meeting began, Amanda reached out to her Human Resources representative to discuss the issue.

From the conversation, Amanda learned that Joe used to be a top performer and had been considered a rising star in the sales department. However, his performance had been deteriorating for a while and there had been little attempt to intervene by her predecessor. Amanda knew she needed to act, not just because of the obvious mandatory behavior change required from Joe, but perhaps to re-engage an individual who was wasting his potential.

A week after the sales meeting, Amanda met with Joe. She put him on notice that the behavior he exhibited at the sales meeting would no longer be tolerated and strongly suggested he seek assistance from the EAP (Employee Assistance Program). She also told him she hoped to eventually see the Joe from earlier in his career—the person who had not only shown so much ability but was a positive force both professionally and personally.

Fast forward several months after Joe's episode at the sales meeting. He had become sober, his team collaboration skills strengthened, his performance soared, and everyone in Joe's life benefited, including, and most importantly, his family. A short while following Amanda's intervention with Joe, his wife connected with her to say thank you for making such a positive impact within their family. Apparently, Joe's alcoholism had not only been negatively impacting his work, but it had also been a growing negative force in the lives of his wife and children, too. Several years later, Joe successfully retired from the company, thanks in large part to Amanda's role in changing his life. She didn't intervene solely for the organization—from her own personal experience, she knew that the tentacles of alcoholism also stretch into an individual's personal life, adding a second and perhaps more important reason for the intervention. Joe's wife told her as much when she thanked Amanda at Joe's retirement party for everything she did for not only Joe's work life, but their family as well.

This aspect of a Best Boss's impact, how they affect the whole person rather than just the working person, was a pleasantly unforeseen insight from our study as evidenced by the following survey quotes:

> I would thank [my Best Boss] for his on-going support and friendship and want him to know the profound impact he has had on me as a person.

My [Best Boss's] impact was more related to my life in general; how I see business, treat people and seek to maintain a sense of perspective.

I am a better person for having known [my Best Boss]. I treat people the same way he treated me.

As a friend, I remind her how much she means to me and how blessed I was to have her in my life.

Impacting *Lives*

Stress causes health issues. And nothing was more stressful than the year 2020. From contentious politics and societal protests, to economic and mental challenges associated with a worldwide pandemic, stress infiltrated all of our lives. But this kind of stress ebbs and flows with moments in time. However, there are some causes of stress that are ever-present in our lives: Rush hour traffic. Going to the dentist. Raising children. Work. A study by Everest College has shown that 80 percent of Americans are stressed about their job, and, for 75 percent of employees, the most stressful part of their job is their immediate boss. This particular stress is leaving its negative mark on our collective health. In 2009, The Karolinska Institute and Stockholm University found that individuals ran a 25 percent greater risk of suffering a cardiac problem if they worked for a bad manager. Similarly, in 2011, the Baylor University Department of Management discovered that individuals who are treated poorly by their supervisors often take their frustrations out at home on their family, or on less powerful people at work. The 2019 International Journal of Environmental Research and Public Health Journal found that employees who did not trust their boss had a higher risk of having four or more heart attack risk factors.

On the positive side, in 2015 the University of Michigan found six qualities of a healthy workplace culture that directly align with the Best Boss Leadership dimensions, characteristics, and behaviors. They include:

- Caring for, being interested in, and maintaining responsibility for colleagues as friends
- Providing support for one another, including offering kindness and compassion when others are struggling
- Avoiding blame and forgiving mistakes
- Inspiring one another at work
- Emphasizing the meaningfulness of the work
- Treating one another with respect, gratitude, trust, and integrity

In this chapter, we have argued that organizational leadership wedded to Best Boss principles make a positive difference to organizations and individuals alike. This argument leads us ask two intriguing questions:

- Why aren't there more Best Bosses?
- How can we have more Best Bosses?

We will attempt to answer these two seemingly simple questions in the upcoming chapter.

CHAPTER 12

Our Aspiration: More Best Bosses!

By this point in our book, we hope we have prompted you to deeply consider your own leadership style. We have offered up our Best Boss study insights, shared compelling stories, and provided opportunities to self-reflect on how your leadership behaviors align with our Best Boss model. In Chapter 9, we shared some specific ideas about how you can improve your people leadership skills. We considered ending our discussion there, satisfied with the prospect that we had the opportunity to influence many of you to become better individual bosses.

However, while there is nothing wrong with individual-by-individual incremental positive change, we have an additional, more ambitious goal. That is to encourage organizations of all kinds, shapes, sizes, and structures to transform their philosophy on how leaders lead others within their walls. To do this, we will first explore the ways in which an organization can better align and develop their leadership expectations and practices using our Best Boss framework. However, as you will see, there are limitations to how successful these strategies *alone* can be. Moving beyond the individual leader, we will investigate how economic and legal forces impact an organization's decisions concerning leadership. Next, we will explore new thinking by business community leaders regarding the importance of considering the interests of multiple stakeholders versus shareholders alone in determining how companies invest. Finally, we will conclude with a provocation to CEOs and executive leadership on how to build the Best Boss brand within their organization.

PART I

Why Don't We Have More Best Bosses?

Jane is the Senior HR VP for a large regional bank, and she was sharing the leadership challenges facing the organization. During the conversation, the topic of Best Bosses came up and she recounted her own personal story. When asked how many senior leaders at the bank possessed the qualities of her Best Boss, she thought for a second, then answered candidly: "One ... and everyone wants to work for him."

Jane's story supports our hypothesis that working for a great boss tends to be the exception and not the rule during one's career. Far too often, the employee/manager relationship isn't all that it could be. So, to answer the question of why we don't have more Best Bosses, the first place to look would seem to be organizational design factors such as strategy, structure, process, rewards, and culture.

Strategy

The link between people leadership and business strategy must be clearly established for an organization to be consistently committed to the development of the Best Boss leadership philosophy and practice. Otherwise, accountability for leadership development will ebb and flow with bottom line results. A long-range plan and an annually implemented leadership development strategy will accelerate the blossoming of Best Boss behaviors and potentially impact the bottom line in a positive way. Furthermore, a statement of leadership philosophy that is conceptually tied to the organization's strategy and success can add even more impetus to the ongoing development of an organization's leaders, and hence, a culture of Best Bosses.

Coauthor John recalls helping an industry-leading multinational consumer products company address this precise issue. The European business unit conducted a succession planning readiness audit across half a dozen countries, and determined that the number of "ready later" and "unlikely to ever be ready" replacements across many business functions in each country far outnumbered "ready now" and "ready soon" candidates. On top of that, competing organizations were snatching up bachelor level and MBA graduates, as well as experienced managers, at an alarming rate. As a result of these internal and external factors, the growth goals of the organization were in serious jeopardy due to the lack of succession bench strength within middle and upper levels of management.

To address this need, the company devised a pan-European leadership development strategy that addressed managerial role definition (to make leadership development an explicit requirement), skill development (including coaching and career development skills), visible and continuing senior executive support, and enhanced communication, recognition, and rewards to acknowledge progress and success. Not only did this strategy deliver the leadership talent necessary to meet the growth needs of the European organization, the strategy was subsequently adopted and successfully implemented by North American business units as well.

Structure

There are a variety of ways to think about "structure" within an organization, and how it can affect the presence or absence of great leaders of people. For example, through short-sighted job and organization design, many bosses suffer from time constraints and/or large spans of control that discourage or prevent them from taking the time to develop meaningful relationships or conduct coaching activities with their direct reports.

We might also think of "structure" in terms of the existence of overarching models or programs that are intended to guide the path and development of leaders in general. Consider that, in many organizations, the best functional performers become supervisors—for example, the best engineer becomes the engineering supervisor, the best accountant becomes the accounting supervisor—often with disappointing results as it pertains to leading people. This is because such supervisors frequently lack preparatory training, experience, knowledge, and skill, not to mention role models for outstanding people leadership.

Charan, Drotter, and Noel (2011) support this notion by arguing that many organizations focus too much of their career mobility and succession planning efforts on promoting individuals with functional expertise, and don't pay enough attention to people with leadership capability:

> Organizations promote people with the expectation that they have the knowledge and skills to handle the jobs rather than the knowledge and skills to handle a particular level of leadership. They assume that if they've performed well at one job, they'll likely perform well at the next one. (Charan, p. 5)

To address this continuing error and what they perceive as a leadership deficit in general, the authors proposed a "leadership pipeline" process model that requires the delineation of skill requirements, time applications, and work values associated with each passage to successive levels of leadership (rather than positions) in an organization. In this model, employees making the passage from individual contributor to first-time manager, for example, "learn how to reallocate their time so that they not only complete their assigned work but also help others perform effectively… they must shift from 'doing' work to getting work done through others" (Charan, p. 17).

Process

Top tier leadership development organizations institute a strong competency-based talent review process to help managers calibrate the performance and potential of those managing employees at the level below them, according to predetermined and comprehensive criteria. In turn, they systematically make decisions about who is ready for promotion, needs further development, or possibly termination/reassignment. These organizations then integrate a strategically aligned, well-planned, fully invested, and robust leadership development process into the mix. Unfortunately, there are far too many organizations that allow the rise and fall of company profits to diminish their talent/leadership development process. These organizations do not view leadership development as a strategic imperative that's a "need to win," but more as a "nice to have" initiative that only receives investment when times are good.

Reward Systems

Organizations understandably focus on tangible business results when rewarding individual or team performance. However, rewards based only on "hard" results can produce leadership behaviors that may be paradoxical to Best Boss behaviors. Based on our study and personal experiences, we would argue companies that successfully integrate "soft skill" people results—like learning and development, potential identification, coaching/mentoring, and communication—into their leadership reward structure will be better positioned to drive continued superior performance. Through our extensive work in organizations, we also have observed the futility, and often cynicism-inducing practice, of incorporating people-focused rhetoric in vision and values statements *without* the hardwiring of supportive practices, processes, and specific behaviors to the organization's reward systems.

Author Duncan recalls two examples from his corporate HR experience that successfully produced individual rewards and recognition based on both tangible and intangible results. One organization incorporated a "values multiplier" into their leadership bonus structure, where the 'hard results' bonus would be multiplied by a percentage of anywhere from 80 to 120 percent based on how well they "lived" the corporate values. A second organization used a "right result, right way" matrix to assess individual performance that equally assessed results *and* behaviors in the calculation of both salary increases and readiness for promotion. In both examples, a clear message was sent to leaders on the importance of balancing results with how they were achieved. A leader who accomplished top results but was a poor people manager was equally at risk as a values-based leader who did not achieve results.

Culture

Organizational culture evolves over time, beginning with the views and values of the founders, then seasoned and enriched by the collective experience. The leadership persona of an organization typically assumes the characteristics and views of the leader in chief, and thus manifests itself within the organizational culture. Predominant themes in organizational cultures, such as focusing on financial and operational results to the exclusion of people results, may discourage an emphasis on "Best Boss" behaviors, particularly if such themes are the mantra of the CEO.

Conversely, the leadership personality of the top executive can have a deep and positive impact on the organization's leadership culture. One example of this is our earlier story describing CEO Peggy Troy's influence on the culture at the hospital. Not only does her behavior impact her direct reports, it appears to impact multiple levels of leadership, and therefore the entire culture of the organization. Time and time again, we've seen the leadership persona in an organization take on the characteristics and views of the leader in chief, and so whatever those characteristics are matters exponentially, as they manifest in the guiding culture of the organization.

We enthusiastically endorse the efforts to use strategy, structure, process, rewards, and culture to promote effective leadership. We further suggest that nonexistent or ineffectively designed strategy, structure, process, rewards, and culture help explain the scarcity of Best Bosses in modern organizations. However, we do not believe this represents the root cause of the issue, and so we persist in asking "why" at least once more.

Why do so many organizations perpetually tolerate deficient or missing structures, processes, reward systems, or cultural characteristics that in turn suppress the development or natural occurrence of great leaders? We contend it is due to powerful internal and external forces that dictate the relentless focus on short-term results that overall please the shareholder at the expense of the employees and other external stakeholders. Interestingly, there is an emerging point of view on the part of researchers and business leaders that the practice of sacrificing the long-term for the short-term achievement of business results might be conceptually flawed in nature. To explore that thinking, let's investigate how economic and legal forces impact an organization's decisions concerning the development of its leaders.

Impact of Traditional Corporate Governance and Corporate Law

In their 2017 *Harvard Business Review* article, "The Error at the Heart of Corporate Leadership," Joseph Bower and Lynn Paine argue that the decades old agency theory of corporate governance is worthy of deliberate and serious debate as a model for the management and governance of today's companies. Simply defined, agency theory is

> a principle that is used to explain and resolve issues in the relationship between business principals and their agents. Most commonly, that relationship is the one between shareholders, as principals, and company executives, as agents. (Investopedia 2021)

The authors explain that the idea of maximizing value for shareholders (principals) should be a fundamental goal sought by corporate managers and assured by company directors (agents) can be traced back to theories put forth by academic economists in the 1970s. One example is the University of Chicago's Milton Friedman, whose views became well-known in the 1970 *New York Times* article, "The Social Responsibility of Business is to Increase Profits." The authors also explain that this "goal" would be considered obligatory, since at the center of agency theory is

> the assertion that shareholders own the corporation and, by virtue of their status as owners, have ultimate authority over its business and may legitimately demand that its activities be conducted in accordance with their wishes. (Bower and Paine 2017, p. 4)

As described in the following, Bower and Paine take significant issue with this premise, and instead, begin to describe an alternative model of corporate governance that is more balanced between the interests of the shareholders and those of the company:

> The agency model's extreme version of shareholder centricity is flawed in its assumptions, confused as a matter of law, and damaging in practice. A better model would recognize the critical role of shareholders but also take seriously the idea that corporations are independent entities serving multiple purposes and endowed by law with the potential to endure over time. And it would acknowledge accepted legal principles holding that directors and managers

have duties to the corporation as well as to shareholders. In other words, a better model would be more company centered. (Bower and Paine 2017, p. 4)

What other flaws exist that potentially lead to the rarity of Best Boss leadership? In his book, *The Living Company*, Arie de Geus (1997) speaks to the preponderance of short-lived companies, in contrast to those that have lasted for literal centuries. Four defining features of long-lived companies were identified, including one which relates conceptually to the community feeling that is engendered by the Best Boss. Long-lived companies were found to be "cohesive, with a strong sense of identity" (De Geus p. 6). No matter how diversified, all company members, and sometimes even suppliers, felt a sense of community and that they were part of something bigger than themselves. De Geus explains that except for when the company was in crisis mode, the top management priority was the health of the institution as a whole. Such strong bonds serve an organization well during challenging times.

Community is defined as a feeling of fellowship with others, as a result of sharing common attitudes, interests, and goals. Let us point out that it is this same feeling of fellowship that develops in the relationship between a Best Boss and direct report—and that trusting relationship is what unlocks the cycle of positive performance and intense engagement that follows as exemplified by the following Best Boss study quote:

> He made me believe in myself more than I thought possible and validated the positives. He also made me feel important— important to our firm, to our team and to him. While I was his subordinate, he made me feel like his partner almost all of the time. He also made me feel like it was fine to be myself. We enjoyed many discussions on many topics and, over time, our professional relationship turned to friendship. This was born of mutual respect and a connection formed by successful experiences in our work... I never wanted to let him down.

De Geus goes on to explain that companies die when the true nature of the organization—that of a community of humans—is ignored, and instead, the focus of managers and shareholders is riveted to the "economic activity of producing goods and services" (De Geus, p. 3). Furthermore, living companies will grow in number only when they are set up according to the same principles that form the basis for human development. De Geus goes on to suggest that without deliberate changes in governance, short-term orientation on profits will continue, and that the culprit behind this may be anachronistic in nature.

> The shareholder-manager relationship may not express corporate reality very well, but it is embedded in the law. As such, the law is an anachronism. It is yesteryear's write up of the situation before World War II, where capital was a scarce resource that deserved special protection and management attention to optimize its use. (De Geus, p. 181)

In conclusion, "maximizing shareholder value" as a management mandate is an almost universally held perspective today. By virtue of its definition, it is easy to understand how various organizational priorities and budgeted initiatives will come and go with the rise and fall of profits. Unfortunately, the systematic and ongoing development of an organization's leaders to properly lead its own people *and* the alignment of related strategies, structures, processes, reward systems, and culture fall into this category. Based on what we have learned and experienced about Best Bosses, this seems so tragic and unnecessary for employees and organizations alike.

The answer to the question "Why Don't We Have More Best Bosses?" seems both obvious and out of sight. Now is a good time to pose and fully answer that question—perhaps better than ever before—as we try to adjust to the rapidly changing workplace due to the environmental, societal, and public health issues that confront us. With that said, we will now dive into the new thinking by business community leaders regarding the importance of considering the interests of multiple stakeholders versus shareholders alone in determining how companies invest.

PART 2

Hope on the Horizon

Interestingly, the writing of this book coincides with recent, pivotal developments in the world of business—developments that will influence the way organizations view the social responsibility of business. We believe, in turn, that these developments will create more opportunity for the ongoing and focused development of leaders—including Best Bosses.

One such development comes from the Business Roundtable (BR). As described on their website as of February 6, 2021, the BR is a nonprofit association based in Washington, D.C., whose members are chief executive officers of nearly 200 major U.S. companies. Together with policy makers, workers, and communities, the leaders of the BR have a mission to strengthen the U.S. economy and its competitiveness and to create jobs through their research and advocacy efforts.

Periodically issuing Principles of Corporate Governance since 1978, the BR has endorsed principles of shareholder primacy (i.e., shareholder interests are a first priority among all stakeholders) in versions they have issued since 1997. However, in an August 2019 press release, the BR announced the release of a new Statement on the Purpose of a Corporation, signed by its 181 CEOs, with a dramatically different focus. They now advocate that corporations have a commitment to *all* stakeholders—customer, employee, suppliers, communities and shareholders alike—and their purpose is to promote a U.S. economy that serves one and all.

Executives in the Business Roundtable provided insightful rationale for this change. Jamie Dimon, Chairman of the BR and Chairman of JPMorgan Chase & Co. explained "the American dream is alive, but fraying... Major employers are investing in their workers and communities because they know it is the only way to be successful in the long term." Alex Gorsky, Chairman and CEO of Johnson & Johnson and Chair of the BR Corporate Governance committee commented that the new statement "... affirms the essential role corporations can play in improving our society when CEOs are truly committed to meeting the needs of all stakeholders." This change comes with the idea that stakeholder interests are inseparable. In other words, an organization cannot successfully sustain itself for the long term when its "success" leads to the downfall of one or more stakeholders, as when the burning of fossil fuels contributes to the acceleration of global climate change, and in turn, harms humanity. BR leaders also took this opportunity to encourage investors to support companies focused on managing the long term, as well as the short term, by investing in the needs of employees among other stakeholders. We believe this opens the door for a more deliberate focus on strategic leadership development, including that of the Best Boss. See Table 12.1 for a Key Excerpt in the Statement of Purpose of a Corporation, released to the public on August 19, 2019.

In another recent development, it is interesting to point out that the 50-year anniversary of *The New York Times Magazine*'s September 13, 1970 publication of Milton Friedman's famous article took place as we wrote this very chapter. In recognition of this milestone, *The New York*

Table 12.1 Key excerpt in the statement of purpose of a corporation

While each of our individual companies serves its own corporate purpose, we share a fundamental commitment to all of our stakeholders. We commit to:

- Delivering value to our customers. We will further the tradition of American companies leading the way in meeting or exceeding customer expectations.
- **Investing in our employees. This starts with compensating them fairly and providing important benefits. It also includes supporting them through training and education that help develop new skills for a rapidly changing world. We foster diversity and inclusion, dignity and respect.**
- Dealing fairly and ethically with our suppliers. We are dedicated to serving as good partners to the other companies, large and small, that help us meet our missions.
- Supporting the communities in which we work. We respect the people in our communities and protect the environment by embracing sustainable practices across our businesses.
- Generating long-term value for shareholders, who provide the capital that allows companies to invest, grow and innovate. We are committed to transparency and effective engagement with shareholders.

Each of our stakeholders is essential. We commit to deliver value to all of them, for the future success of our companies, our communities and our country.

Source: https://businessroundtable.org/business-roundtable-redefines-the-purpose-of-a-corporation-to-promote-an-economy-that-serves-all-americans

Times collaborated with DealBook to "revisit the legacy" of Friedman's essay by sharing excerpts of it along with reactions of its impact from modern day CEOs and economists. While Friedman's essay still has its proponents, we have captured in Table 12.2 some dramatic protestations of modern leaders whose remarks were published in the September 13, 2020 publication.

Table 12.2 Some reactions to the Friedman Doctrine 50 years hence

Milton Friedman: "In a free-enterprise, private-property system, a corporate executive is an employee of the owners of the business. He has direct responsibility to his employers. That responsibility is to conduct the business in accordance with their desires, which generally will be to make as much money as possible while conforming to the basic rules of the society, both those embodied in law and those embodied in ethical custom."	Marianne Bertrand, professor of economics at the University of Chicago Booth School of Business "The shareholder-primacy view of the corporation… has been the modus operandi of United States capitalism. Why did this view become so dominant? One rationale was a practical one. Rather than being asked to balance multiple, often conflicting interests among stakeholders, the manager is given a simple objective function. More important, though, was the naïve belief, dominant in the Chicago school at the time, that what is good for shareholders is good for society—a belief that rested on the assumption of perfectly functioning markets. Unfortunately, such perfect markets exist only in economics textbooks."
Milton Friedman: "The Social Responsibility of Business Is to Increase Its Profits"	Marc Benioff, chief executive of Salesforce "I'll never forget reading Friedman's essay when I was in business school in the 1980s. It influenced—I'd say brainwashed—a generation of CEOs who believed that the only business of business is business. The headline said it all. Our sole responsibility to society? Make money. The communities beyond the corporate campus? Not our problem." I didn't agree with Friedman then, and the decades since have only exposed his myopia. Just look where the obsession with maximizing profits for shareholders has brought us: terrible economic, racial and health inequalities; the catastrophe of climate change."

Source: https://nytimes.com/2020/09/13/business/dealbook/milton-friedman-essay-anniversary.html

So, it seems there might never be a better time to use momentum such as this to think through what it is that your organization can do, specifically, to influence the development of Best Bosses. To achieve this will provide great dividends for all stakeholders.

Detailed proposals for delving into your organization's leadership development strategy and process are beyond the scope of this book. However, what can be done—regardless of where your organization stands at this time—is simply to start the conversation. That is where all good change begins. To facilitate this dialogue, we conclude this chapter with an "Open Letter to Our CEO" you can use as a template to address the development of Best Boss behavior within your organization.

Open Letter to Our CEO

Dear CEO,

As the individual who has risen to lead our organization, we invite you to reflect upon the people who were most helpful to you in your career journey. Most importantly, who was the Best Boss you ever had? Why do you see him or her in this way? What did he or she do? How did this boss make you feel? What was the impact of his or her leadership on your career? Recent research provides this "thumbnail sketch" of the five determinants of Best Boss leadership:

Demonstrating an interest in the direct report beyond immediate performance (i.e., **Leads from a Higher Purpose**), the Best Boss discerns and takes steps to **Activate Potential**, **Promote Dynamic Autonomy** and independent action-taking, and then **Provides Pervasive Feedback** and **Inspires Continuous Learning** in ways that make positive impacts on the motivation, job performance, career development, and even the personal life of the employee.

The truth is, this finding is backed by decades of research and evidence on the positive impact of leaders who exhibit these behaviors—on every-thing from engagement and performance, to retention, careers, and even personal lives. Abundant research also evidences the detrimental impact of "bad boss" behavior—not just the toxic impact on the aforementioned, but also the harmful impact on emotional adjustment and health.

Whether or not you personally have had that Best Boss experience, we urge you to consider the benefits our organization stands to gain in having as many **leaders of people** as possible develop and demonstrate more effective skills in these five dimensions, and to quickly take stock of our readiness and capability to deliver on this aspiration. Do we collectively lead our organization in a way that takes into consideration the dramatic impact that effective leadership can have on our people and in turn, our organization as a whole? If it does, how much time, attention, and resource do we invest at this time to identify, develop, deploy, and reinforce Best Boss behavior? Here are fourteen (**14**) determinants that are key indicators of readiness. We believe challenging our organization to gauge their current extent of use of these determinants will provide the most powerful starting point:

1. **Organizational Culture:** To what extent do you and our Board of Directors integrate Best Boss elements into our mission and values, define an explicit leadership "brand," and expect senior executives set the example through their behavior?

2. **Vision:** To what extent does our organization have a philosophy of leadership that details what is expected of those who lead people, and why it matters?

3. **Strategy:** To what extent does our organization have an explicit strategy, plan, budget, and progress measures to develop leaders?

4. **Structure and Work Arrangements:** To what extent do we ensure that span of control and the work situation provides the supervisor opportunities to observe and interact informally with direct reports?

5. **Recruitment and Selection:** To what extent do we seek to hire, select and/or promote supervisors whose skills and traits are consistent with the Best Boss behavior model?

6. **Performance Management of Employees:** To what extent do we ensure that clear expectations, feedback, coaching, explicit linkage between performance and rewards, etc. are integral to the employee experience through the efforts of the person to whom he or she reports?

7. **Performance Management of Those Who Lead Others:** To what extent do we require that, in addition to providing employees the above performance management elements, supervisors are expected to address the professional development of their employees and seek upward feedback from direct reports?

8. **Succession Planning/Talent Management:** To what extent are individuals who display Best Boss leadership skills taken into account when identifying succession planning candidates for critical leadership positions within the organization?

9. **Rewards:** To what extent are leaders throughout the organization rewarded for their people leadership results?

10. **Organization Communications:** To what extent do we utilize social and print media, upward or 360-degree feedback, employee surveys, town hall meetings, etc., to communicate expectations, ensure two-way communication, and track our progress with respect to Best Boss behavior and impact?

11. **Leadership Development:** To what extent do we train people leaders in critical Best Boss skills such as questioning and listening, strategic thinking, emotional intelligence, etc.?

12. **Career Development and Succession Planning:** To what extent do we explicitly define job mobility requirements and processes, and ensure supervisors are actively supporting employee career development?

13. **Technology:** To what extent do we have in place a technology-enabled competency structure and career development structure and process, along with technology-enabled online training programs to support employee performance and career development?

14. **Measures, Metrics, and Milestones:** To what extent does our organization assess progress in leadership development and the impact of improved leadership on organizational performance?

Becoming a Best Boss organization will not happen overnight. We will need to deploy or achieve a critical mass of these determinants to move forward. Your assessments not only provide important benchmarks of our "current state" of readiness; in addition, these replies provide an element-by-element gap analysis between our current state and the "desired future state" of being a Best Boss organization.

Can we count on your leadership and support to amplify the processes that will help bridge the gap between current and desired states, and move us forward to being recognized internally and externally as a Best Boss organization? You can count on my [our] efforts to support yours.

CHAPTER 13

Lees' Story: A Millennial's Perspective

How much of it was it the time in my life and how much of it was his doing? I'm not sure. But he gave me the ability to trust myself by (always) making me feel valued. I knew that I mattered, not only as an employee, but as a person.

By all accounts, Lees appeared to be an adventurous and confident young woman. Her early life journey took her from a small Canadian village on British Columbia's Vancouver Island to Montreal's McGill University, and then off to London with her college sweetheart, Jeremy, who was pursuing his master's degree at the UK's Royal School of Music. All of this happened before she was 25 years old.

Lees' young life unfolded in ways that seemed ordinary to her at the time, but in truth, are quite remarkable. And, as with many of us, events from her life were providing her clues regarding her special gifts, talents, and potential. As a teenager, she worked at the world-renowned Sooke Harbor House, where the owner trusted her to serve their most important celebrity patrons. She graduated from one of Canada's most prestigious universities. Upon moving to London, she landed a job at the famous Gaucho Restaurant, a massive structure sprawled across four floors facing the Piccadilly Circus in the heart of London. Lees was initially hired as a receptionist, but within six months she was promoted to the position of Events Manager. An amazing £1 million were earned for the events conducted during her brief time in this role. While these are noteworthy achievements, Lees was unsure of herself personally, and her professional direction was also unclear to her. But fate would soon intervene, thanks to a Best Boss she seemed destined to meet.

It was clear other people had seen something in me, but I always missed it for one reason or the other. I did not take ownership.

Once the master's degree was completed, Lees and Jeremy moved back to Chicago where he grew up. Both of them needed jobs. Two companies and two interviews later, Lees was hired by Vantage Leadership Consulting to support a partner, two consultants and run the reception desk. It was during her tenure at the firm that Mike Tobin became Lees' Best Boss.

When Lees started her role, she was experiencing some major personal issues in her life. Her mother had just been diagnosed with cancer and died within one year. Six months later, she and Jeremy became engaged. Around this time, Mike took Lees out to lunch, but the conversation was not about work. It was personal. How was she dealing with the loss of her mom? How were her brother and father doing? How could Mike help her and Jeremy get their future life off to a great start?

He took such an unexpected and unnecessary interest in me, (not only as an employee), but as a whole person.

As her boss, Mike took a special interest in helping Lees understand and appreciate her inherent talents. Mike's focused approach and unique style were instrumental in helping her internalize his coaching and mentoring.

He made me realize that I wasn't just the best of the mediocre options. That I was actually… that I had opinions. He used to say that I was too hesitant about expressing my insights and thoughts … he actually chided me for being what he called a "squeaky baby secretary"—when I tried to insert myself into a discussion. And he was right. My face would turn bright red and voice would trail off and disappear as I tried to share my thoughts with others. When I displayed this behavior, he would always call me out and constantly told me to stop underselling myself. He would tell me, "You are more and better than you know. You just have not figured it out yet."

I can remember talking in a meeting and there he was with his hand behind his ear, helping me by encouraging me to speak up and speak out. He would talk to me later on and give me feedback. I heard you or I didn't hear you at the end of your point. He would say, "I'm an old man and I need to hear you!" He was constantly challenging me like that but made it so low risk. He made it like a joke. It came with such support I knew that it came from a place of love.

Within two years, Lees had moved beyond the receptionist desk and became Mike's primary administrative support. Yet, just as in many of her prior roles, Lees found herself doing much more for the firm beyond her stated responsibilities. Mike responded by engaging her in a series of conversations about her interests and what other talents she might bring to the firm as a whole. As a result of Mike's continued encouragement and queries about her interests, she was able to articulate an attraction to marketing. Once her desire was uncovered, Mike asked Lees to create a business plan and define how she could play a role in helping the firm advance its marketing capabilities. Mike then brought this information forward to the other partners and advocated on her behalf. Encouraged by their support, she obtained a Marketing Certificate from Cornell, paid for by Mike and the firm. Eventually, Lees was promoted to Marketing Director and went on to make substantial contributions in the design and execution of marketing activities for the firm.

He 100 percent supported me... He helped me recognize my value.

Who knows what direction Lees' life would have taken had she not found her way to Vantage and had the opportunity to work for a Best Boss? But she did. And her Best Boss had a profound and lasting impact, not only on her work and career, but also on her life.

The things that Mike showed me about myself are invaluable. The confidence I have to speak up and speak my opinion—that is really important, and I wasn't able to do that... He changed my life... I'm sure he helped me become a better person.

Appendix

Best Boss Action Planning and Actualization Example

The Case of Chris

Introduction

Chris is a recently hired accounting supervisor in the Finance department of a mid-sized corporation. Chris received a bachelor's degree in accounting with a minor in math from a respected Midwest university, and was hired prior to graduation by one of the "Big Four" public accounting firms. After working for three years as a public accountant and earning the Certified Public Accountant (CPA) certification, for family reasons, Chris returned to the family's home town and took this corporate position.

In this new position, Chris has been assigned supervisory responsibilities for eight employees, ranging from new college graduates to long-term high school graduate clerical employees. Although Chris was an individual contributor and not a supervisor in the Big Four firm, the CPA certification and work experience were considered sufficient preparation by the new employer for becoming a supervisor in accounting. While it may be possible for Chris to get some training in management and leadership in the future, business conditions do not permit that investment at this time.

As a bit of an introvert, Chris did not aspire to elected office in the college's Accounting Society, but was active in many community services projects such as youth tutoring, Habitat for Humanity, and charitable activities sponsored by the university chapel. Being concerned about potential gaps in leadership know-how and skill, Chris researched the topic, found the Best Boss book, read it, and decided to embark upon the recommended action planning and leadership actualization process.

These notes present the key highlights of Chris' analysis and action planning, to assist the reader in navigating his or her own leadership voyage.

Paired-Comparison Evaluation Matrix for Frequency of Use of Best Boss Behavior Dimensions

Chris used the "Quick Self-Assessment" approach described in Chapter 9 to complete an initial evaluation of current extent of use of the five Best Boss behavior dimensions, utilizing the matrix presented in Figure 9.1. Chris' choices (indicated by brackets) and scoring are presented below:

	Leads from a Higher Purpose	Activates Potential	Promotes Dynamic Autonomy	Provides Pervasive Feedback	Inspires Continuous Learning
1	[Leads from a Higher Purpose]	Activates Potential			
2		[Activates Potential]	Promotes Dynamic Autonomy		
3				[Provides Pervasive Feedback]	Inspires Continuous Learning
4	[Leads from a Higher Purpose]		Promotes Dynamic Autonomy		
5		Activates Potential		[Provides Pervasive Feedback]	
6			Promotes Dynamic Autonomy		[Inspires Continuous Learning]
7	Leads from a Higher Purpose			[Provides Pervasive Feedback]	
8		Activates Potential			[Inspires Continuous Learning]
9			Promotes Dynamic Autonomy	[Provides Pervasive Feedback]	
10	[Leads from a Higher Purpose]				Inspires Continuous Learning
Total Choices	3	1	0	4	2
Rank Order 5= highest 1 = lowest	4	2	1	5	3

Based upon this self-assessment, Chris decided to focus on two of the Best Boss dimensions—Promotes Dynamic Autonomy and Activates Potential. To take the analysis to the next step, Chris went back to the Self-Reflection scales for these two dimensions, and completed them:

Chris' Promotes Dynamic Autonomy Self-Reflection

III.	Promotes Dynamic Autonomy: On a 5-point extent of use scale: To what extent do you typically exhibit this behavior?				
	Not at All	To a Small Extent	To Some Extent	To a Moderate Extent	To a Large Extent
	1	2	3	4	5

Instructions: Using the scale above, write the number in the space to the left of each survey item that best represents your current use of the behavior. Next, calculate the average score and fill in the result in the space provided. At your option, you may use this information in Chapter 9, How to Become a Better Boss.

4	Set clear expectations for direct reports in the "what" and "how" of getting their job done
2	Provide direct reports the autonomy to do their job in the best way they can
1	Help direct reports achieve a "big picture" view of the business and organization
4	Explain the work standards you expect direct reports to achieve
1	Teach direct reports to work productively through organizational politics
2	Take steps to improve direct reports' understanding of how the organization operates—both formally and informally
2	Help direct reports understand the business the organization is in and their role within it
1	Encourage direct reports to think and act strategically
2	Share a vision of what you want to achieve
4	Set clear goals and objectives for direct reports' work performance
2.3 (fill in average)	Average Extent of Use: Promotes Dynamic Autonomy

Chris' Activates Potential Self-Reflection

II.	Activates Potential (On a 5-point extent of use scale: To what extent do you typically...)				
	Not at All	To a Small Extent	To Some Extent	To a Moderate Extent	To a Large Extent
	1	2	3	4	5

Instructions: Using the scale above, write the number in the space to the left of each survey item that best represents your current use of the behavior. Next, calculate the average score and fill in the result in the space provided. At your option, you may use this information in Chapter 9 ("How to Become a Better Boss.")

4	Offer direct reports opportunities to show what they can do
4	Treat direct reports as individuals with talents to contribute, regardless of job title or pay level
2	Serve as an advocate for your direct reports to perform up to their best potential
2	Place your direct reports in situations that "showcase" their talents and allow others to recognize their talents
2	Supportively "push" your direct reports to achieve outside of their comfort zone
3	Encourage your direct reports to bring forth their recommendations and ideas
2	Demonstrate that you value your direct reports' views through acting on their ideas
2	Identify challenging situations and deploy direct reports to them so as to accelerate their development
2	Identify and address organizational barriers that potentially could hinder the development of direct reports
2	Identify and address self-imposed barriers that may impede the performance and development of direct reports
2.5 (fill in average)	Average Extent of Use: Activates Potential

Analysis of Self-Reflection Ratings

Chris was not pleased with the patterns evident in these replies. The Dynamic Autonomy ratings evidenced fair strength in conveying expectations and standards, but far less attention to developing direct reports' understanding of the bigger picture and the political dynamics of the company. The need to pay better attention to explaining context and encouraging more autonomous action was clear. The Activates Potential ratings were also mixed. While direct reports were certainly being treated fairly and given the opportunity to show what they could do, the emphasis seemed to be on "here and now" performance, to the exclusion of identifying and taking advantage of opportunities to develop direct reports' potential.

Overall, these ratings indicated to Chris that, thus far, a number of key leadership ingredients related to the engagement and performance of direct reports were being overlooked, and, the development of direct reports was largely being ignored. Specific opportunities to provide better leadership were clear, and the potential for improvements in engagement, performance and development was abundant. These insights and the detailed ratings then set the stage for action-planning.

Chris' Best Boss Action Planning and Actualization Worksheets

Action Objectives and Plan

> *Step 1*: Based on your self-assessment and review in this chapter, please identify between two and three of the most important areas for development and write the dimension titles in the following chart.
> *Step 2*: Next, for each dimension chosen, identify up to three of the lowest-rated behaviors in the respective dimensions.
> *Step 3*: For each prioritized behavior, create a weekly action plan using the forms provided.

	Priority	Top Priorities for Development
	Dimension title	Lowest rated dimension behaviors (up to 3 per dimension)
1	Promotes Dynamic Autonomy	Help direct reports achieve a "big picture" view of the business and organization
		Teach direct reports to work productively through organizational politics
		Share a vision of what you want to achieve
	Dimension title	Lowest rated dimension behaviors (up to 3 per dimension)
2	Activates Potential	Supportively "push" your direct reports to achieve outside of their comfort zone
		Identify challenging situations and deploy direct reports to them so as to accelerate their development
		Identify and address organizational barriers that potentially could hinder the development of direct reports
	Dimension title	Lowest rated dimension behaviors (up to 3 per dimension)
3		

Chris' Plan for Week One

Behavioral objective	What I plan to do this week
From the Priority List above, choose a low-rated behavior to address this week and write it in the space below:	Get specific on what you plan to do as it pertains to this behavior:
Dimension title: Promotes Dynamic Autonomy Behavior: Share a vision of what you want to achieve	Who: All direct reports What: Meet in order to explain my vision for our work group and plan for helping them develop better understanding of the business and the company Where: Conference room When: Thursday morning 10 a.m. to noon Why: Provide context and direction for the work group and begin to demonstrate a higher standard of leadership

Learning partner	Supportive stakeholders	Contingent reward for success	End of week Self-rating 10=HIGH; 1=LOW
Who will be your learning partner for this objective that will observe you in action and provide feedback?	Who will you identify as key stakeholders for moral support?	How will you reward yourself if you make notable progress this week?	Based on input from others and your own self-observation, how would you rate progress on this objective?
Will enlist Lee, my most-trusted direct report and alum of my Big Four firm, to observe and provide candid feedback	Will enlist my supportive spouse to provide moral support. Will "test" level of moral support available from my boss, the Director of Accounting	Will indulge in a caloric "guilty pleasure" (e.g., visit donut shop or malt shop)	To be determined

Behavioral objective	What I plan to do this week
From the preceding Priority List, choose a low-rated behavior to address this week and write it in the space below:	Get specific on what you plan to do as it pertains to this behavior:
Dimension title: Activates Potential Behavior: Supportively "push" your direct reports to achieve outside of their comfort zone	Who: All direct reports What: Begin individual one-on-one meetings with all direct reports Where: Conference room When: Schedule one meeting each day until completed Why: Get a better sense of current skill set and direct reports' own views of their comfort zone and areas for expansion and development

Learning partner	Supportive stakeholders	Contingent reward for success	End of week Self-rating 10=High; 1=Low
Who will be your learning partner for this objective that will observe you in action and provide feedback?	Who will you identify as key stakeholders for moral support?	How will you reward yourself if you make notable progress this week?	Based on input from others and your own self-observation, how would you rate progress on this objective?
Will enlist the company's HR Director to serve as a "sounding board" for progress and problems, as well as provide information on available training and development opportunities	In addition to my devoted spouse, will seek moral support from the HR Director	Will indulge myself with a two hour visit to the gym (will help offset both stress and caloric indulgence previously mentioned)	To be determined

Chris Completes Remaining Self-Reflection Scales and Profiles All Five Best Boss Dimensions

Completion of Self-Reflection Scales

Buoyed by the insights emerging from completion of the Dimension II and III scales, and pleased by the progress being made in implementation of action plans, Chris decided to complete the detailed self-reflection ratings for the remaining three dimensions. The resulting averages from Chris' replies are presented in Appendix Figure A.1.

CHRIS' INITIAL SELF-ASSESSMENT PROFILE

	Value
Leads from a Higher Purpose	3.9
Activates Potential	2.5
Promotes Dynamic Autonomy	2.3
Provides Pervasive Feedback	3.4
Inspires Continuous Learning	2.8
Overall Average Extent of Use	2.98

Chris' initial self-assessment profile

These scores confirm the priority that Chris has given to Dimensions II and III, highlight the relative strength of Dimensions I and IV, and also provide a strong initial or premeasure of Chris' starting point in this improvement journey. At some future date, Chris may complete the self-reflection scales a second time, to provide a postmeasure of progress.

Conclusion

We trust that sharing some of the details of Chris' journey brings both realism and optimism to your own leadership development efforts. Small, focused and sustained changes in behavior can have a big impact in your work and in your life, as well as in the work and lives of your direct reports!

Best Boss Blank Forms

RESULTS FOR:_____   DATE:_____

Leads from a Higher Purpose

Activates Potential

Promotes Dynamic Autonomy

Provides Pervasive Feedback

Inspires Continuous Learning

Overall Average Extent of Use

0   0.5   1   1.5   2   2.5   3   3.5   4   4.5   5

Best boss dimension extent of use profile

Paired-comparison evaluation matrix for frequency of use of best boss behavior dimensions

	Leads from a Higher Purpose	Activates Potential	Promotes Dynamic Autonomy	Provides Pervasive Feedback	Inspires Continuous Learning
1	Leads from a Higher Purpose	Activates Potential			
2		Activates Potential	Promotes Dynamic Autonomy		
3				Provides Pervasive Feedback	
	Inspires Continuous Learning				
4	Leads from a Higher Purpose		Promotes Dynamic Autonomy		
5		Activates Potential		Provides Pervasive Feedback	
6			Promotes Dynamic Autonomy		Inspires Continuous Learning
7	Leads from a Higher Purpose			Provides Pervasive Feedback	
8		Activates Potential			Inspires Continuous Learning
9			Promotes Dynamic Autonomy	Provides Pervasive Feedback	
10	Leads from a Higher Purpose				Inspires Continuous Learning
Total Choices					
Rank Order 5= highest 1 = lowest					

Action Planning and Actualization Forms

Step 1: Based on your self-assessment and review in this chapter, please identify between two and three of the most important areas for development and write the dimension titles in the chart below.

Step 2: Next, for each dimension chosen, identify up to three of the lowest-rated behaviors in the respective dimensions

	Priority	Top priorities for development
	Dimension title	Lowest rated dimension behaviors (up to 3 per dimension)
1		
	Dimension title	Lowest rated dimension behaviors (up to 3 per dimension)
2		
	Dimension title	Lowest rated dimension behaviors (up to 3 per dimension)
3		

> *Step 3*: For each prioritized behavior, create a weekly action plan using the forms provided

Plan for Week _____

Behavioral objective	What I plan to do this week
From the Priority List above, choose a low-rated behavior to address this week and write it in the space below:	Get specific on what you plan to do as it pertains to this behavior:
Dimension title: Behavior:	Who: What: Where: When: Why:

Learning partner	Supportive stakeholders	Contingent reward for success	End of week Self-rating 10=High; 1=Low
Who will be your learning partner for this objective that will observe you in action and provide feedback?	Who will you identify as key stakeholders for moral support?	How will you reward yourself if you make notable progress this week?	Based on input from others and your own self-observation, how would you rate progress on this objective?

References

2000 *"Annual Report." Fairfield, CT: General Electric Company. 2001.* https://annualreports.com/HostedData/AnnualReportArchive/g/NYSE_GE_2000.pdf

Abbajay, M. September 7, 2018. "The Negative Health Consequences of a Bad Boss." *Harvard Business Review*, Retrieved from https://hbr.org/2018/09/what-to-do-when-you-have-a-bad-boss

Alterman, T., R. Tsai, J. Ju, and K. Kelly. January 15, 2019. "Lack of Trust in a Manager can cause Cardiovascular Disease." *International Journal of Environmental Research and Public Health*, Retrieved from IJERPH | Free Full-Text | Trust in the Work Environment and Cardiovascular Disease Risk: Findings from the Gallup-Sharecare Well-Being Index (mdpi.com)

Alvero, A.M., Buckland, B.R., and Austin, 2001. "An Objective Review of the Effectiveness and Essential Characteristics of Performance Feedback in Organizational Settings. (1985–1998)." *Journal of Organizational Behavior Management* 21, no 1, 3–29, http://doi.org//10.1300/J075v21n01_02

Anderson, J., and D.A. Level. July 1980. "The Impact of Certain Types of Downward Communication on Job Performance." *Journal of Business Communication* 17, no. 4, 51–59. http://doi.org//10.1177/002194368001700405

Balcazar, F.E., M.K. Shupert, A.C. Daniels, PhD., T.C. Mawhinney, PhD., and B.L. Hopkins. 1989. "An Objective Review and Analysis of Ten Years." *Journal of Organizational Behavior Management* 10, no. 1, 7–37, http://doi.org//10.1300/J075v10n01_02

Bower, J.L., and L.S. Paine, L.S. 2017. "The Error at the Heart of Corporate Leadership." *Harvard Business Review*. Reprint 1703B, Published in HBR May-June 2017, pp. 2–12.

Brooks, M., J. Stark, and S. Caverhill. 2004. *Your Leadership Legacy: The Difference You Make in People's Lives.* Berrett-Koehler Publishers.

Business Roundtable. August, 2019. "Business Roundtable Redefines the Purpose of a Corporation to 'Promote and Economy that Serves All Americans.'" Press Release retrieved from https://businessroundtable.org/business-roundtable-redefines-the-purpose-of-a-corporation-to-promote-an-economy-that-serves-all-americans

Carlson, D.S., M. Ferguson, P. Perrewé, and D. Whitten. November 20, 2011. "The Fallout on Family Members and Subordinates stemming from an Abusive Supervisor." *Personnel Psychology*. Retrieved from https://onlinelibrary.wiley.com/doi/abs/10.1111/j.1744-6570.2011.01232.x

Charan, R., S.J. Drotter, and J. Noel. 2011. *The Leadership Pipeline: How to Build the Leadership-Powered Company.* San Francisco: Jossey-Bass.

Csikszentmihalyi, M. 1990. *Flow: The Psychology of Optimal Experience.* New York, NY: Harper and Row.

Curtin, M. 2019. "Empowering and Engaging Employees By Listening to Them." *Inc.* Retrieved from https://inc.com/melanie-curtin/employees-who-feel-heard-are-46x-more-likely-to-feel-empowered-to-do-their-best-work.html

Deci, E.L., and R.M. Ryan. February 14, 2008. "Facilitating Optimal Motivation and Psychological Well-Being Across Life's Domains." *Canadian Psychology* 49, no. 1.

de Geus, A. 1997. *The Living Company.* Boston, Mass: Harvard Business School Press.

Dweck, C. 2016. *Mindset: The New Psychology of Success.* New York, NY: Ballentine Books.

Friedman, M. September 13, 1970. "The Social Responsibility of Business Is to Increase Its Profits." *The New York Times Magazine,* pp. 122–126.

Gallup, Inc. 2017. *State of the American Workplace.* Washington, DC.

Gallup, Inc. 2017. "An In Depth Look at what Characterizes Great Managers." Retrieved from The State of the American Manager.

Gallup, Inc. 2020. *State of the American Workplace.* Washington, DC.

Garelli, S. 2021. "Why you Will Probably Live Longer than Most Big Companies." https://imd.org/research-knowledge/articles/why-you-will-probably-live-longer-than-most-bigcompanies/#:~:text=A%20recent%20study%20by%20 McKinsey,S%26P%20500%20will%20have%20disappeared (accessed February 5, 2021).

Gladwell, M. 2018. *Outliers: The Story of Success.* New York, NY: Little, Brown & Co.

Greenleaf, R.K. 1970. *The Servant as Leader.* Cambridge, Mass: Center for Applied Studies.

Harter, J., and A. Mann. 2017. "Common Philosophies of Highly Engaged Corporations." *Gallup,* Retrieved from https://gallup.com/workplace/236366/right-culture-not-employee-satisfaction.aspx

Hogan Assessments Systems, Inc. 2014. "Stress Is Killing You." Retrieved from https://hoganassessments.com/wp-content/uploads/2014/08/Stress_Health_eBook_Final.pdf

Investopedia. 2020. "Agency Theory." Last modified January 27, 2021. https://investopedia.com/terms/a/agencytheory.asp

Kilts, J. 2007. *Doing What Matters: How to Get Results That Make a Difference - The Revolutionary Old-School Approach.* New York, NY: Crown Publishing Group.

Kim, D. 1993. "The Link Between Individual and Organizational Learning." *MIT Sloan Management Review*, https://news.stanford.edu/2019/09/30/embrace-struggle-education-professor-challenges-common-beliefs-teaching-learning/

Korkki, P. April 23, 2011. "The Shifting Definition of Worker Loyalty." *New York Times,* https://nytimes.com/2011/04/24/jobs/24search.html

Lazear, E., and K. Shaw. 2012. "The Value of Bosses." *National Bureau of Economic Research,* Retrieved from https://nber.org/system/files/working_papers/w18317/w18317.pdf

Maslow, A. 1943. "A Theory of Human Motivation." *Psychological Review* 50, no. 4, 370–396. http://doi.org//10.1037/h0054346

Mayo, E. 1945. *Social Problems of an Industrial Civilization.* Boston: Graduate School of Business Administration, Harvard University.

McGregor, D. 1960. *The Human Side of Enterprise.* New York, NY: McGraw-Hill.

Pink, D. 2009. *Drive: The Surprising Truth About What Motivates Us.* New York, NY: Riverhead Books.

Schwantes, M. September 7, 2018. "Toxic Bosses can Impact Your Health." *Inc.*, Retrieved from https://inc.com/marcel-schwantes/research-says-working-for-these-4-types-of-toxic-bosses-can-ruin-your-health.html

Seppala, E., and K. Cameron. December 01, 2015. "The Effects of Positive Practices on Organizational Effectiveness." *Harvard Business Review,* Retrieved from Proof That Positive Work Cultures Are More Productive (hbr.org).

Spears, L.C. 2010. "Character and Servant Leadership: Ten Characteristics of Effective, Caring Leaders." *The Journal of Virtues & Leadership* 1, no. 1, 25–30. https://regent.edu/wp-content/uploads/2020/12/Spears_Final.pdf

Spector, C. 2019. "'Embrace the Struggle': Stanford Education Professor Challenges Common Beliefs about Teaching and Learning." *Stanford News,* September 30, 2019. https://news.stanford.edu/2019/09/30/embrace-struggle-education-professor-challenges-common-beliefs-teaching-learning/

Zenger, J., and F. Joseph. January 15, 2014. "Your Employees Want the Negative Feedback you Hate to Give." *Harvard Business Review.* https://hbr.org/2014/01/your-employees-want-the-negative-feedback-you-hate-to-give

About the Authors

Duncan Ferguson has an extensive background in corporate human resources and in depth organizational consulting experience. He provides executive coaching, leadership development counsel, career advice, and thought leadership to an array of clients and colleagues (dferguson@ vantageleadership.com).

Toni M. Pristo, PhD, is an organizational psychologist assisting organizations in leadership and organization development. Founder of Pristo Consulting in 1996, her mission is to develop moral leadership that optimizes the potential of employees, businesses, and society (toni@pristoconsulting.com).

John Furcon assists business and governmental organizations in achieving successful transformation and executive development. He has served as a principal at Harbridge House, PricewaterhouseCoopers and Buck Consultants, and program director at The University of Chicago (johnfurcon17@gmail.com).

Index

OTHER TITLES IN THE HUMAN RESOURCE MANAGEMENT AND ORGANIZATIONAL BEHAVIOR COLLECTION

- *Emotional Connection: The EmC Strategy* by Lola Gershfeld and Ramin Sedehi
- *Civility at Work* by Lewena Bayer
- *Lean on Civility* by Christian Masotti and Lewena Bayer
- *Leaderocity* by Richard Dool
- *Agility* by Michael Edmondson
- *Strengths Oriented Leadership* by Matt L. Beadle
- *Leadership In Disruptive Times* by Sattar Bawany
- *The Successful New CEO* by Christian Muntean
- *Level-Up Leadership* by Michael J. Provitera
- *Chief Kickboxing Officer* by Alfonso Asensio
- *Transforming the Next Generation Leaders* by Sattar Bawany
- *Breakthrough* by Saundra Stroope
- *Women Leaders* by Sapna Welsh and Caroline Kersten
- *The New World of Human Resources and Employment* by Tony Miller

Concise and Applied Business Books

The Collection listed above is one of 30 business subject collections that Business Expert Press has grown to make BEP a premiere publisher of print and digital books. Our concise and applied books are for...

- Professionals and Practitioners
- Faculty who adopt our books for courses
- Librarians who know that BEP's Digital Libraries are a unique way to offer students ebooks to download, not restricted with any digital rights management
- Executive Training Course Leaders
- Business Seminar Organizers

Business Expert Press books are for anyone who needs to dig deeper on business ideas, goals, and solutions to everyday problems. Whether one print book, one ebook, or buying a digital library of 110 ebooks, we remain the affordable and smart way to be business smart. For more information, please visit www.businessexpertpress.com, or contact sales@businessexpertpress.com.

www.ingramcontent.com/pod-product-compliance
Lightning Source LLC
Chambersburg PA
CBHW050500190326

41458CB00005B/1366